AN INVESTIGATOR'S LIFE

by

Louis J. Ruchek

Binford & Mort Publishing
Portland, Oregon

I want to especially thank my family from the bottom of my heart. I recognize and appreciate their many personal sacrifices when I was unable to be with them evenings, on weekends and holidays.

An Investigator's Life

Printed in the United States of America

ISBN: 0-8323-0543-X

Library of Congress Catalog Card Number: 00-111525

First Edition 2001

CONTENTS

PREFACE

Evidence is the heart of a trial. Without good evidence, the most successful trial attorney will fail. As a result, trials are won or lost during the investigation phase, when evidence is obtained and preserved,. In our legal system, the principle form of evidence is the testimony of a witness. Lou Ruchek was and is the master at locating and obtaining accurate statements from a witness.

The first case I worked on with Lou was a murder case, which went to trial in Hillsboro. On the other side, the prosecutor was the head district attorney, who the paper lauded, upon his retirement, as one of the great Oregon trial attorneys. Behind the prosecutor was his office staff of investigators as well as three detectives, one of whom was a forensic scientist. In addition, the prosecutor had the use of unlimited deputies and policemen to perform detail work. On our side, we had Lou Ruchek. Looking back on it, we had the clear advantage. The young man was acquitted of murder, as he should have been.

It is difficult for a legal investigator to get a witness to talk, especially in a murder case. However, Lou never seemed to have difficulty in accomplishing this task. The real reason that witnesses opened up to Lou was because he was scrupulously honest and had impeccable integrity. Those qualities shown on him and, as a result, people naturally trusted him.

In my view, juries do not always understand or follow the law. They do understand and base their verdicts on common sense. Lou Ruchek was an outstanding investigator because he had the same common sense and instinctively knew how a jury would react to a piece of evidence. Another of Lou Ruchek's many traits is his ability to write. He has always been an interesting storyteller. At one time, I encouraged him to write a book about some of his interesting cases. However, I did not anticipate the scope of quality of this book. In the vernacular, it is a "very good read."

Anthony W. Furniss
Attorney at Law
Portland, Oregon
October 5, 2000

Occasionally extraordinary personal insight can be gleaned from glimpses of the life of a common man or woman with uncommon sense and a rare ability to relate to other people. While Lou Ruchek was invaluable as a skilled claims handler and private investigator extraordinaire, he was also key to the success of many trial lawyers, based upon his ability to deeply listen to others and an uncanny nose for the truth. his interpersonal skills made him a friend and confidante of those he worked for, managed and taught as well as his adversaries. Reading about his successes and failures provides a personal opportunity to see humility, perseverance, loyalty, trust and friendship at the highest level. After reading his book you, too, will want to ask him to coffee and enrich your life with some of his memorable stories.

Austin W. Crowe, Jr.
Attorney at Law
Perkins Coie, LLP
October 23, 2000

INTRODUCTION

These are the stories of a father and his son. The father, Joseph Ruchek, was a skilled barrel maker who emigrated to the United States of America from Czechoslovakia at the turn of the century and, through hard work and sheer determination, became a successful businessman. His son, Louis J. Ruchek, inherited all the best qualities of his father, added some of his own, and went on to have a successful career as an investigator for the Union Pacific Railroad and, after retirement, as a private investigator.

The tales may be simple, but the telling is honest and sincere. The love, pride, and deep respect that Louis has for his late father and for all that his father taught him is obvious.

Sit back and enjoy reading about times gone by. Don't be surprised if you find yourself comparing life then and now.

Lou states, "I went from a child growing up on a farm in Beaverton, who swam in a stream with a beaver named Roger, to a grown man racing back to his car with a barking, snapping Rottweiler just inches from the seat of my pants. Here's how I got there."

MY FATHER, JOSEPH RUCHEK

My father, Joseph Ruchek, was born in Bulsho, Czechoslovakia, in 1884. He was one of seven children. His father, a veterinarian, worked around the flat countryside treating animals for all types of sicknesses and injuries.

When my father was a small boy, he would ride with his father from farm to farm to treat the animals. They traveled in a one-horse drawn cart with huge six-foot wooden wheels, identical to the one shown in the farm scene in Van Gogh's famous painting, "Vegetable Garden" (1888).

On one occasion, my father watched as his father plunged a long sharp knife into a specific spot in the side of a cow that had eaten too much clover. The animal was down and near death in a bloated condition. A few minutes after the knife had entered, the cow was up on her feet casually eating clover again as though nothing had happened. My father pointed out that, although my grandfather was very busy, being a veterinarian was not a lucrative profession. The peasants were very poor and money was a real problem for them. Nevertheless, my father said his family always had plenty to eat because my grandfather was usually paid for his services with a goose, chickens or an occasional piglet. My grandfather was well known in the countryside and, as a professional man, often assisted in making village decisions.

My grandfather once treated an animal for a farmer who did not have any money. To pay his debt, he gave my grandfather an old bible. That bible, which is now about 400 years old, was brought to this country by my father at the turn of the century. Other than some clothes, the bible was one of the few possessions my father had when he landed in New York as an immigrant. The bible, which was well read by my father is in good condition and is now kept in a vault for safekeeping. It is written in the Czechoslovakian language and was copied by a Catholic Bishop for peasants to give as a Christmas present to the baron whose land they farmed. My father told me that back then the bibles were copied by church officials for the wealthy who could read and write.

My father was one of the few youngsters who completed grade school, at a time when it was quite common for children to be put to work at an early age. When my father was seven years old it was his duty to milk a cow before and after school, as well as feed the poultry and the animals.

When he was twelve, he was sent to a winery in Budapest to learn the trade of a cooper (barrel maker). This was actually a skilled profession. In those days big and small barrels were most commonly used to contain liquid substances.

My father hardly ever drank water during his four-year apprenticeship—the water was not purified. From age twelve, until he died at ninety-three, he drank a glass (or two) of wine a day—one with lunch and one with dinner. When I was a boy there was always wine on the dinner table. If my brother, sister or I wanted a glass, all we had to do was pour it for ourselves. We rarely did.

My father told me that when he was about fourteen years old that the owner of the winery took him in a horse-drawn wagon to a mountainside where wine had been stored for 150 years. He tasted some of the wine that had been boiled down from an ice-like cube. Although he only took several small sips, he almost passed out when he stepped into the sunlight.

When he was an apprentice learning the trade of a cooper he actually disliked the occupation. He had always wanted to build and create structures. One day, several bricklayers were building a shed at the winery. When they went to lunch, my father (who was about thirteen) was fascinated with the brickwork and proceeded to lay bricks on their unfinished walls. When the bricklayers returned from lunch they noticed the walls were several feet higher than when they left. They recalled that a young boy had been watching them lay the bricks, but they thought it could not have been him because of the professional way the bricks had been laid. Yet, who else could it have been? When they asked my father, he admitted that he had laid the bricks. The bricklayers were so impressed with the rows of brick my father had added, that they told the owner of the winery that my father was in the wrong occupation and that he should be trained to be a bricklayer. The man then wrote my grandfather and told him that even though his son was doing well as a cooper, he should be a bricklayer as he showed real talent for that craft. My grandfather wrote back saying that he did not want his son to be a bricklayer, he wanted him to learn the trade of a cooper. That ended the subject, and my father continued his study and work as an apprentice barrel maker.

It is astonishing that a youngster in those days could not choose his profession, but had to follow the wishes of his parents. There were no ifs, ands or buts about it—the parents had the final say.

Being a cooper was an art. Barrels were made to contain liquids, and a cooper who made leaky wooden barrels was simply not tolerated. My father sustained many burns to his hands when learning the profession as the iron hoops had to be hot when placed on the barrels.

There were about twenty-five boys in the barrel-making school. They came from all over Europe, even as far as Sweden. Except for my father, who was the youngest, all the boys were in their middle teens. After working six ten-hour days they had one day off. The work was strenuous and tiring and the apprentices went to bed early. They were required to go to church on Sunday, and after service, the remainder of the day was their recreational time. It was on those Sunday afternoons that my father would go to the countryside or walk over the huge chain link bridge between the cities of Buda and Pest. He said that when soldiers marched over the bridge they had to break cadence because the bridge would rock back and forth when they marched in precision. Upon completion of his barrel-making training, my father was an accomplished cooper, and was given a certificate and a card to present to future employers. He always carried his cooper card throughout his travels in Europe and in America.

After receiving his cooper papers, my father considered enlisting and becoming a Hungarian Cossack. The Cossacks were fierce fighters and considered more elite than the Russian Cossacks. My father was eager to travel and he had heard that the pay was good for barrel makers—particularly for someone who could repair barrels. He decided to go to an army facility for more information, where he was told that he would be given a certain rank for enlisting. Coopers were always assigned to the cavalry units because barrels of water were hauled on carts to and from battlefields to water the horses and men. My father was told that even though he would spend most of his time working on barrels, he would also have to be a horse soldier. He went to the arena where the recruits were being trained to ride their spirited mounts. He thought the inductees were fortunate not to be required to begin training with their sabers at their sides because many of them fell off their horse. A training officer whipped a recruit when he fell off his horse. This was supposed to "encourage" the recruit to make a better effort to stay on. When my father saw several of the men were beaten, he decided (with tongue in cheek) that army life was not for him. He was told the officer whipped the trainee to see if he would come back—proving he had a lot of determination that would make him a good soldier. In any event, he had a change of heart about joining the cavalry unit, and placed his thoughts of work elsewhere.

My father was an adventurous person. He had spirit, a restless nature and a strong desire to see and do everything. After the army episode, he decided to tour Europe—mostly on foot—with a Swedish youth who also had completed cooper training at the winery. They started out with their cooper's identification cards in their pockets and their tools strapped on their backs.

The two young coopers would go to the nearest village, call on business establishments and ask if barrels needed repair. They would earn enough money to pay for food and a bed to sleep in. Occasionally they took a stagecoach as they went from place to place. Working their trade, they kept busy with work from city dwellers, as well as from farmers who saw them walking on the dusty roads, and who asked them to repair their barrels. Going from village to village, they worked their way through Hungary and through many other countries. The larger cities usually had many cooper shops and were well supplied with coopers. When they were in the countryside, they asked the farmers if they would let them sleep in the barn for the night. Usually, the farmer had barrels waiting to be repaired. There were streams where they would bathe whenever the opportunity presented itself. They bathed religiously, no matter how cold it was. The two young men were hardy people and seldom had colds.

My father told a story about being between villages when it was beginning to get dark. The next village was quite a distance away so they stopped at a farmhouse and politely asked the farmer if they could sleep in his barn. The farmer agreed and later came into the barn and invited them to dinner with his family. The meal consisted of one item, a bowl of real hot Hungarian goulash—a ragout of beef or veal, flavored with red-hot paprika and vegetables. My father was accustomed to this type of very spicy dish, but his companion, the Swedish youth, was not. It would have been impolite not to eat, so the young Swede did the best he could—eating the hot goulash, while wiping the tears from his eyes. The farmer's wife noticed the crying young man and asked my father about it. My father could not say, of course, that the hot goulash caused the tears because this would have insulted the hosts. Thinking quickly, he replied that his companion had received news that very day that a member of his family had died. In response, the farmer's wife said, "Oh, the poor boy, the poor boy. I am going to give him another bowl of goulash." The Swedish youth, not being able to speak Hungarian very well, wondered what was going on and why he was being given another bowl of goulash when he could hardly finish the first one. Later, the farmer's wife came to the barn and brought a warm blanket for my father's companion. Since she did not bring my father one, the young man asked my father why he was getting so much attention from the farmer's wife. When my father failed to answer, the Swedish youth thought she possibly found him good-looking and perhaps had a crush on him. In addition to furnishing the blanket, the farmer's wife invited them to finish the goulash for breakfast the next morning. My father told his companion they were invited back for breakfast the next morning to finish the goulash. The young man said his stomach was still upset and as far as he was concerned, he was out of there. They arranged to meet down the road later after my father had finished his goulash breakfast.

The two young coopers worked in several villages and were able to observe many local customs. They worked in the vineyards and wineries of Hungary and the wine country on the rocky slopes of the Rhine River in Germany. They particularly enjoyed Sundays because that was the day for church. They always made it a point to be in a village to attend church as well as the dancing festivities in the afternoons. My father said they were treated royally because the villagers looked upon them as hard-working and skilled craftsmen, particularly my father who was only sixteen. To be a certified cooper at that young age was quite an accomplishment.

After many months of traveling they finally ended up in Hamburg, Germany. At this point, the Swedish youth wanted to go back to Stockholm, and my father decided to return to Bulsho.

My father talked with many sailors in Hamburg while he repaired water and wine barrels for the sailing ships. The German sailors, who had sailed for many years all over the world, told stories about wonderful America, and agreed that if they had a choice, they would first go to America, and second to Hawaii. It was at this time my father made up his mind that he was going to America, and if he could not accomplish that he would go to Hawaii. He returned home and wrote to an aunt in Buffalo, New York, to sponsor him to come to America.

His entry was arranged, and he arrived as an immigrant in New York at Ellis Island at the turn of the century. He was seventeen years old; he was alone, and he would never return to his homeland.

My father said coming over to this country as a third-class passenger was rather rough, but he was excited to be in a new world that was full of opportunities and work. Being studious in nature and wanting to be a part of this country, he spent all of his spare time studying the English language and reading books. In a short time he was able to read and write English. He often said that one of the greatest days of his life was the day he obtained his citizenship papers.

It was not long before he left Buffalo and traveled to Chicago, where he took a job at a meat packing plant making barrels for meat and lard. He had found that his skill as a cooper made it easy for him to obtain a job and, more important, the pay was very good. He worked with an African-American assistant named Adam and the two became good friends. Adam told my father that he wanted to go back home to the south to visit relatives whom he had not seen for many years.

Shortly thereafter, the two men left Chicago and headed for Virginia taking their tools for barrel-making with them. When they reached the south, their money ran out and they traveled from town to town, mostly on foot, working part-time as coopers.

One very hot day, they were trudging through the countryside when they came to a small town. They were thirsty and stopped at a saloon. My father asked the bartender, who turned out to be the owner of the saloon, if they could have a drink of water. The bartender said my father could have water to drink but, looking at Adam, the bartender pointed to a spittoon on the floor and said if he wanted a drink that he could drink out of the spittoon. My father replied that if his companion could not have a drink of water, he did not want one either, and he and Adam walked out of the saloon thirsty.

They had left the town a mile or two behind them when a man in a buggy overtook and stopped them. It turned out that he was the sheriff of the town they had just left. He told them he had a report that they were two wise guys and had insulted a citizen in the town. He told them that they would have to return to town and go to jail. My father explained that they were not looking for trouble and suggested that if the sheriff had any barrels that needed repair that they would do the work for free. After thinking it over for some time, the sheriff agreed.

My father thought that repairing a few barrels was a lot better than spending time in a jail or time on a chain gang. The sheriff took him at his word and they not only repaired barrels for him, but also for his brother, aunt, uncle, grandfather, etc. My father said he'd never known anyone to have so many relatives. To add insult to injury, they also had to work on the bartender's barrels and on the wooden spokes of his wagons.

My father intensely disliked the racial discrimination in this country. In Europe he had found little, if any.

After leaving the town, Adam told my father that there were bad men in the south, but that all men were not bad. He said that although his father and grandfather were slaves the plantation owner treated them well. He took care of them and saw to it that they had plenty of food, a roof over their heads and good medical care. They were not mistreated. Adam said that when he was a boy, the plantation owner saw to it that he learned to read and write. Adam explained to my father that there were good bosses and mean and nasty bosses.

The two broke up their travel arrangement because Adam wanted to stay in the south, and my father wanted to see what was going on in the State of California. Upon arriving in California, he worked at various wine barrel shops. He then traveled to Seattle, Washington, where he replenished his money belt by working on wine barrels for sailing ships. Later, he continued north into Alaska where he worked in fish canneries that packed salmon into barrels. Alaska wasn't to his liking and he returned to Portland, Oregon. My father had liked what he saw in Portland when he was passing through on his way to Alaska. He went to work for the Knight Pickling Company in St. John.

At this time, my father heard that there were homestead rights being issued to anyone who was a citizen, and who would go into the timber country around Seaside, Oregon. The amount of land he could acquire from the government was one quarter of a section—160 acres. Under the Homestead Act Law, on January 1, 1863, any citizen could file for a quarter section of free land, and would own the land after five years. To comply with the Act you had to build a house, dig a well and clear ten acres. It also required that care had to be given to ten acres of timber.

My father's section was located about six miles from Seaside, Oregon, had a beautiful stream running through, and an incredible stand of virgin timber between 300-400 years old. The butts of some of the huge Douglas firs were six to eight feet in diameter—a car could be driven through the butt of the tree if a hole were cut in the tree's trunk. Being able to own land was very important to my father because in old Europe it was almost impossible to be a landowner. He liked the idea that after living on the timber acreage for five years it would belong to him. Homesteading changed my father's life. Instead of working on barrels, he found himself building a cabin, sheds and a smokehouse.

My father built his cabin near the Nehalem River. He would walk about six miles through the forest to Seaside to buy his supplies and pick up his mail. He told me that, although it was a lonely life, he enjoyed the forest and the animals. In the winter, he would stay in his cabin and read books in front of a roaring fire. He would take his .30-.30 rifle, walk to the river, shoot a salmon in the shallow waters, and then smoke the big fish in his smokehouse. Besides taking trips to Seaside to repair barrels, he would take some of the smoked salmon and trade it for supplies. There were so many salmon in the river that he would catch them and use them for fertilizer.

On rare occasions, he would take the train to Portland and spend the day shopping, returning home in the evening. While in Portland on one of these shopping trips, he passed a music store and saw and heard a phonograph playing music for the very first time. The phonograph, about two-feet-square, had a picture of a dog on the speaker and a handle to wind it to play the record. These were the first phonographs for sale in the area and my father was so fascinated with what he saw and heard that he immediately purchased one. He paid for the music box and records with gold coins he had saved for emergencies. He carried his purchase to the train station and returned to Seaside. He strapped the phonograph on his back and proceeded to walk through the timber six miles to his cabin. He had one neighbor between Seaside and his cabin, and when he arrived at his neighbor's house, he just had to show him what he had bought. The neighbor was positively amazed when my father started playing the record of band music. The two of them then came up with the idea to play the music near the barn where the neighbor's wife was milking the cow. They hid themselves in the brush by the barn and my father began loudly playing a band number out into the wilderness. The next thing they knew, the cow panicked upon hearing the music blaring, kicked over the milk bucket and ran out of the barn at full speed with the neighbor's wife following right behind. She was absolutely mystified at hearing a marching band playing in the remote wilderness. After catching the cow, she proceeded to give my father and her husband a good scolding. We still have the phonograph and it is still in good playing condition.

My father told an interesting tale that went back to his childhood days in Czechoslovakia. When he was about ten years old, it was his job to take the lunches his mother made out to the woodcutters his father employed. On one particular day he started out with four lunches in sacks for the woodsmen. He was early and as he walked through the woods he came to a little stream. Because he had some time, he placed the food by a tree trunk and proceeded to play in the creek until he finally decided to go deliver the lunches. He went back to the tree where he had left the lunches and, to his amazement, he could not believe his eyes—the lunches were gone. He looked all around the area of the tree, but he could not find them. He then ran back to his mother, who spanked him for losing the lunches. The men were able to eat when he finally arrived with the second batch of lunches, but he was criticized for being late.

Approximately ten to twelve years passed and one night, when he was sleeping in his cabin, he dreamed of the stolen lunch incident. He said that in his dream he saw himself placing the lunches near the tree and, while playing near the water's edge, he saw a man mirrored in the water stealing the lunches. The man was known in my father's village.

Later that morning, my father decided to go to Seaside to get supplies and pick up his mail. He walked the six miles to the post office and had a letter from his mother. In the letter she told him that the man he had seen mirrored in his dream stealing the lunches had died but, before he died, had confessed to my father's mother that he had taken the lunches. Apparently, this act was on his conscience and he wanted it known before he died. My father was very perplexed and could not fathom why, after more than ten years, he would have a dream revealing the man involved and on the same day receive a letter from his mother identifying that same man as the one responsible for the theft of the lunches. Was this a coincidence—the dream and the letter on the same day?

After staying the required number of years, my father obtained ownership of the timberland in 1910. He then returned to Portland where he went back to work for the Knight Pickling Company. After working about one year—the longest period of time he had worked for one company—he wrote a letter to my mother who had already made entry into this country and was living in Chicago. My mother and father were schoolmates in grade school. They were married in Chicago and both came to Portland where my father had purchased a house in the Mt. Scott area.

Although he worked and lived in Portland, he continued to own and pay taxes on the Seaside homestead property until World War II, at which time he sold the timberland, including the cabin he had built. He sold the property because he was always afraid of fire. This fear was enhanced by news that the Japanese were attempting to place fire bombs in the forests along the West Coast.

lso, in 1933 there was a huge forest fire in the Pacific Coast Range named the "Tillamook Burn" which incinerated more than 250,000 acres of virgin timber. It was one of the largest forest fires on the North American Continent. I was about twelve years old at the time of the fire, and remember

Photo-Art Commercial Studios Photo No. 22452665

Early logging train on a bridge made from some of the local timber.

it well. Even though our farm was about 100 miles away, the fire was so intense that the skies were dark with black billowing smoke—even during the daytime. I remember being frightened as we watched cinders drop around us.

Four giant fires occurred before my father sold the timber. It is estimated that thirteen billion board feet of timber burned in these fires and about one-half of that was salvaged because the flames did not burn entirely through the trees. Because of the fires, my father was afraid he might be next to suffer such a terrible loss. He sold the land and timber to a forest products company. Had he held the property for five to ten more years, he would have been a millionaire many times over. However, my father, like always in his life, never looked back. "What is done is done," was his favorite saying.

My father got up at half past four in the morning in order to get to his pickling company job by seven o'clock. He traveled to work by streetcar and had to make three transfers to get to the factory in St. John. He never complained about his long commute because he used the time to read and improve his English.

He worked for a number of years at the pickling factory after which he saved enough money to buy thirty acres about one-half mile from the center of Beaverton. The acreage consisted of about twenty acres of fruit trees and about ten acres of bottomland that at one time—a long time ago –had been the bottom of a lake. When we were children we found arrowheads in the bottomland which indicated that many years before Indians lived on the edge of the lake. My father loved trees, and my parents were happy with the purchase. In the middle of the bottomland there was a good-sized creek which was supplied from a giant spring that was located about one-half mile from my father's land.

He made a down payment on the land with the intention of selling apples from the nearly 500 trees on the farm. The former owner of the land who sold it to my father boasted around Beaverton that he had received a very good down payment, but that it would only be a matter of time before he would get his farm back. He was of the opinion that payments could not be made from the sale of apples. He never failed to point out that the three previous buyers could not make the payments and each time the farm was returned to him. He did not believe that it would be any different with my father.

As it turned out, my father had an apple crop failure the very first year. Not only did the crop fail, but many of the trees froze because of the severe cold that winter. Prospects were dismal and it appeared that, unfortunately, the seller of the land was going to make good on his prediction that the farm would come back to him.

My father went to Mr. Knight, the owner of Knight Pickling Company, to discuss the matter. Mr. Knight thought a lot of my father, not only because he was an excellent cooper and a hard worker, but also because he brought considerable publicity to the Knight Pickling Company at barrel-making contests. The contests were sponsored to determine who was the fastest barrel maker on the West Coast. My father, decked out in Knight Pickling Company colors, was second in every single one of the contests he entered. The contests were held at picnics in different cities and taking second place was quite an honor. My father just could not beat the one cooper who represented a large barrel company in Vancouver, British Columbia. My father said that early on he spoke to the winner who told him that his secret in consistently winning contests was to heat the iron hoops to a point that they had to be handled very fast to prevent burning his hands. After looking at this cooper's thick scarred hands, my father thought that perhaps second place was not all that bad.

Love Apples grew in clusters—at one time my father
shipped 20 tons of these apples to the Orient.
They were sweet and would keep almost forever.

In any event, when my father told his boss that he might lose his farm, Mr. Knight suggested that he raise horseradish for him on the bottomland. He added that my father could arrange to come in and work on special barrel assignments whenever he needed someone to solve a barrel-leakage problem.

After working fifteen-hour days for seven years as a cooper, orchardist and horseradish grower, my father owned the farm lock, stock and barrel. In addition, he had saved almost $5,000, and about a year before the great Depression, he spent most of this money to build a new house—performing much of the work himself. So many of the immigrants who came to this country around this time were bonded by this same admirable trait—hard work. When they got into trouble, they solved most of their problems by working harder and longer.

The farm's apple box label. Used from 1945-1982.

My father was fascinated by a "Lady Apple" tree in the orchard that was brought over by a pioneer prior to 1900. This cute apple is perfectly shaped, red with yellow stripes and is about the size of a walnut. He shipped them to the Orient and to Hawaii where they were very popular and sold at four dollars a pound. The Asians were quite fond of the little apples and considered them a delicacy. The fact that they were a hardy apple and a good keeper in warm weather also contributed to their popularity in the Orient. Sometimes the apples were used for decorations. Dancers in Hawaii took the ones about the size of marbles and placed them in their hair. The mainlanders saw the apples and assumed they were grown in Hawaii. The apples grew in clusters—more or less like grapes, and my father grafted about 150 trees of these Lady Apples. Since the apples were good keepers they could be picked almost in freezing weather.

The apple had three names: Lady Apple, Love Apple and Christmas Apple. My father said the name Love Apple came from France where they originated. The growers of these little red apples with the yellow stripes would build a fire under a black kettle of water, fill it with apples and boil them all night. In the morning, all that would remain would be a honey-like substance at the bottom of the kettle. The fact that teenagers (boys and girls) were required to keep the fire going all night resulted in what fathers termed "hanky panky" which is how one of the names for this apple—"Love Apple"—originated.

The six acres of lake bottomland was not of much value because floodwaters from the creek would remain until early summer, at which time it was too late to plant the early profitable vegetables. This made it difficult to farm the very rich black soil. My father realized the value of farming the land in early spring and set out to drain it. He started building forms to make three-foot concrete tiles—two a day—for two years. After he made a sufficient number of tiles, he used horses to dig out a channel. The tiles were then lowered into the quarter-mile long ditch using a crane that he built. After three years, he completed the project that allowed him to plant early spring crops on the eight acres. This brought him a comfortable income along with his earnings from the orchard.

I was about twelve years old when my father had completed the project and was visited by a government agent who wanted to see what my father had accomplished with the new drainage ditch. After my father had proudly shown him around, the man announced that the government would pay him $150. This was a lot of money during the Depression, and my father asked him why he was entitled to this money when the work merely benefited him. The agent told him about an existing Act that entitled him to this money for turning a swamp into productive land. When my father heard that the money came from the taxpayers, he told the man that he had not put in the tiles so that the taxpayers would pay him. He added that he did not want the payment because the taxpayers did not have anything to do with a project that would

I am the small one at the end, The horse's name was "Dutch" and she saved my life when I was about 2-years old., (1926)

make money for him in the future. It wasn't just my father who felt this way. Thousands of other immigrants who came to this country appreciated that they could work and have a better life—which was payment enough.

In light of my father's ties with the Knight Pickling Company, he started to raise horseradish and sold it to them. Growing horseradish was hard work, but was profitable. The roots are plowed out in the late fall, sometimes in the mud. There was a lady who lived in Beaverton who immigrated from Italy in 1905. Her name was Rose Biggi. She was left alone with three small children in the Depression years with very little money. She started making a living grinding horseradish in the basement of her home. My father sold some of his horseradish to this hardworking woman who eventually built a respectable food business. Her company now employs 100 people and does millions of dollars in business each year. This is certainly a far cry from the modest beginnings of Beaverton Foods selling small jars of horseradish to stores and door-to-door. She, like my father, continued to work right up into her later years.

When my father first started to raise tons of horseradish, a neighbor had to show him how to harness the horses—two powerful grays named Dutch and Chub. Dutch was a mare and was sort of an easy-going horse, but had the strength of two horses. Chub was a little temperamental, but was much smarter than Dutch. Chub was purchased from a dairy that delivered milk to homes by wagon. My father was told that, after a while, Chub would stop at the houses that were supplied with milk without any direction. This was an amazing feat considering the route had more than 100 stops.

In addition to the orchard, raising horseradish and farming other vegetables, my father planted about one-half acre of poppies. In the fall, the bulbs turned brown and the poppy seed inside the bulb was black. The poppies were not raised as a sale crop. My mother used the poppy seeds for making absolutely delicious poppy seed cakes. My father checked with police officials to see if poppies could be grown. He was advised that it was permissible providing he would call them prior to harvest so they could inspect the field. The police had to make sure that the bulbs had not been cut from the stems, indicating that the poppies had been harvested green and were being used for opium. Each year, after they checked the field, my mother invited them for coffee and poppy seed cakes. As I mentioned before, my mother's poppy seed cakes were delicious and it wasn't very long before the police would call several times before the dried poppies were ready to be inspected. Although one official was capable of checking the field, eventually two of them would come out and end up having the cakes and coffee. It must be understood that visitors to our house were always offered coffee or wine and, of course, a treat—like a poppy seed cake. This was a ritual among most of the farm immigrants. A guest simply had to come in and join in a snack.

Although the eight acres of bottomland were very productive, a tremendous amount of work was required to raise garlic, horseradish, onions, and the other vegetables. My father's first love was the apple trees, especially the Love Apples.

Considerable irrigation was required for the production of apples and vegetables. As children, we enjoyed running underneath the sprinklers on a hot summer day.

My father had a ten-horse, gasoline, one lunger engine he started by placing a foot on a spoke and then giving it a hefty kick. That engine could be heard popping as far as the City of Beaverton—a mile away. He had to be very careful when he kicked the three-foot flywheel because at times the wheels would jerk backward, and could have easily broken his leg.

The Farm

When I was absent during World War II, my father raised fifty tons of garlic on the eight acres and was paid a handsome price per pound. The garlic was purchased for seed in California and some of the bulbs were as large as coffee cups. The local newspaper, *The Beaverton Enterprise,* ran an article about my father and referred to him as the "Garlic King."

When I was growing up, Beaverton's business area took up two or three blocks. About three blocks from the city's center, two Greek immigrants operated an eight-acre celery farm. I recall a produce buyer telling my father that those eight acres produced the second best celery grown in the United States, and was recognized for its great taste and, particularly, its enormous size. As a small boy, I played hide and seek in the boarded rows of celery that were as tall as I was. When coming home from grade school the owners would give me two stalks of celery out of their shed to take home. The two stalks were as much as I could carry, and it became a contest for me to try to sneak by their celery shed without being seen—so I wouldn't have to carry the heavy stalks home.

The creek that ran through our farm originated from a large spring in a hill located about one-half mile from my father's place. My father built a three-inch pipeline and the creek supplied irrigation water for us and for about twenty farmers down the line—all raising all sorts of vegetables from lettuce to celery.

In the summertime we would dam the water and, although the water was cold, it was refreshing on those hot summer days. A beaver we named Roger, sometimes joined us while we were swimming. Roger would stick his head out of the water and continually bark at us for invading what he apparently considered his private domain. Trout were plentiful in the stream, particularly closer to the spring. The creek was filled with big crawfish. We didn't eat them when we were growing up because we simply felt they were too ugly. Now, of course, they are considered a delicacy. At times, we would see a mother crawfish making her way up stream in the clear water with five little ones crawling in a line right behind her. They were cute and about the size of a half-dollar.

After my father purchased the farm, he planted quite a few grapes around the house to reinforce his wine supply. Originally, he did not grow enough grapes to make wine so he purchased many boxes of grapes from California during the early years of prohibition. Even though prohibition was in effect, my father did not think he should be out of his wine. He had been drinking wine since he was a young boy learning the cooper trade at the winery. Wine was like water to him. He would make about 100 gallons that would last him for the year. After he made the wine, he contained it in a barrel and hid the barrel in a hedgerow of brush between his property and the neighbor. Because it was illegal, he waited until dark to siphon some of the wine from the barrel into a jug.

One fall day, my father was plowing with horses and the sheriff came up and asked his permission to hunt pheasants on the farm. We had a cornfield and the hedgerow where pheasants were plentiful. The sheriff had hunted our farm before and was always successful in bagging several birds.

After my father gave the sheriff permission to hunt, he walked alongside the hedgerow and, as bad luck would have it, several birds flew up and the sheriff brought one of the birds down. The only problem was that the bird landed in the brush where my father hid his wine barrel. My father ran up to the sheriff and told him he had changed his mind—that there would be no more hunting and that he would have to leave the property immediately. The sheriff said he would leave, but that he would first like to pick up the bird in the brush he had just shot. My father, knowing that there was an excellent chance for the sheriff to find the wine barrel, told him not to pick up the bird.

Years later, after prohibition was voted out, my father told the sheriff why he had ordered him off the property. The sheriff confessed that he had always wondered why my father had changed his mind in such a hurry—allowing him to hunt one minute and ordering him to leave the next. He said that had he discovered the wine barrel the only thing he would have demanded would have been to share a glass of wine with him.

Many of the immigrants had wine in their homes during prohibition. My father was acquainted with two of his countrymen who had wine in their Portland home. These two men heard through the grapevine the police might raid them and confiscate their wine. Even though it was late and quite dark, they hurriedly carried a heavy barrel of wine about a mile from their home to a wooded area, and placed the barrel under a bridge. Later, when they thought the coast was clear, they went to the bridge to retrieve the heavy barrel. Alas, the barrel of wine was gone. When telling my father of their misfortune, one of them commented, " I hope the winos who hit the jackpot and took our wine had a helluva good time—and the headaches to go with it!" My father laughingly told the two men that at least they didn't have to carry the heavy barrel back home. They didn't find his remark particularly amusing.

Finally, my father was cited for having a jug of wine in his home. When he appeared in court, the judge asked him what he had to say for himself. In a very sincere tone, my father explained to the judge that he had grown up drinking wine; that the water was so bad in Czechoslovakia where he lived as a child that drinking wine was common. He didn't think having a glass or two of wine with his dinner every night was any big deal and, he definitely didn't feel it was a crime. Why, he explained, even at the Last Supper of Christ they served wine. My father assured the judge he wasn't selling his wine to anyone, but would occasionally share it with friends at dinner. After listening to my father, the judge found my father guilty and sentenced him to probation. However, in closing, the judge commented, with a grin, that he would like to come over for dinner.

At times, my father and I talked about the advances in medicine since the turn of the century and how fortunate we were to live in a time of such great doctors and scientists. My father said that one day while he was working for the pickling company he felt a real sharp pain in his side. It was so intense that he dropped to the floor. He was immediately taken to a Portland hospital and diagnosed as having kidney stones. Two large male nurses in white uniforms carried him to a room that contained a bathtub filled with steaming hot water. He put his finger into the hot water and told the two nurses that there was no way he was going into the tub no matter what kind of pain he was experiencing. After letting him have his say, they picked him up, placed him in the tub and held him down. He screamed and yelled to be let up. He came to believe the nurses were deaf. Every time he tried to get up, they pushed him back. There were two changes when he finally came out of the bathtub. One, he looked like a red lobster, two, the pain in his side had disappeared.

I told this story to two doctors. One said that it was obvious the heat had dissolved the kidney stones, and the other one said the hot water would have had no effect on the kidney stones. One must give a great deal of credit and praise to today's doctors and scientists for raising the standards of medical care to help reduce pain and suffering.

When my father was about eighty-five years old, he worked in his orchard pruning trees standing on a tall ladder, even in icy weather. The fact that he was on a slippery ladder ten to fifteen feet above the frozen ground did not bother him. I tried to discourage him from performing this kind of work because I was afraid that he would fall and end up in a wheelchair. He retorted that if he could not prune his trees he would just as soon be in a wheelchair.

About a week later, I stopped at the farm on my way home from work. Father was in the kitchen. I sensed that he was not his usual self, but I attributed it to his possibly just having an "off" day and I went home. About two hours later I received a call from him saying that he wanted me to come over to the farm as soon as possible. I rushed there and found him on the kitchen floor in severe pain. He sheepishly told me that he had fallen from a twenty-foot ladder while pruning his trees that afternoon. I took him to the hospital. He had broken four ribs. It wasn't more than three or four weeks after this accident that he was back trimming his trees in icy and rainy weather.

One day when my father was about eighty years old, he was disking the orchard. As he was looking backward at the disk, a low branch of a tree knocked him off the tractor. He fell in front of the moving disk and the sharp blades ran over his back. Fortunately, a neighbor happened to see him fall off the tractor and ran to help. My father was rushed to the hospital with all sorts of cuts on his back. When I heard about the accident, I immediately called the doctor to find out the extent of my father's injuries. I was told that they were going to keep him in the hospital overnight, and the doctor assured me, "He is alright. How can you hurt such a tough old man?" Several weeks later he was back disking his beloved orchard.

One morning I stopped at the farmhouse and drank some well water from the kitchen faucet. It tasted sort of funny, but I brushed it aside because the well had always contained good water. About a week later I stopped in again and discovered that my father was having severe stomach aches. While I was debating whether or not to take him to the doctor, I had a glass of the well water. It really tasted oily, so I called the Fire Department. They came out and tested the water. One of the firemen took a sample of water from the faucet, placed it in a dish, lit a match and *set the water on fire*.

Fortunately, we figured out what tainted the well water. The underground tank that fueled the school buses was located about 300 feet from the well and was leaking into my father's well. He stayed at the hospital for a few days, recovered and returned home. The school paid my father's medical bills and arranged for city water to be piped into his house because his well was ruined.

Another time, my father was walking a cow from a dairy to his farm. As he rounded a curve in the road, a truck appeared, ran off into the shoulder, striking my father and knocking him into a ditch. The cow started to run down the street with the driver of the truck in hot pursuit.

It was amusing to my father that the truck driver was more concerned about the runaway cow than about his injuries. I questioned my father as to what, if any, settlement was made. My father answered that after the accident he was "sitting on the moon", as the settlement was very fair. He said the truck driver performed chores around the farm for a few days and paid the medical bills. Father said he was sore for a few days, but quickly recovered.

My father never forgot his youth or the difficulties he encountered when he was young. He really liked people and would talk with them at night after work for hours. On weekends we would go to the neighbors and visit with them late into the night. This event was always accompanied by a snack, and was our family's entertainment until the time my father purchased a radio.

My father raised hay during the Depression. He provided tons of hay to nearby farmers who sometimes didn't pay him for six months or a year later. In those days, however, a bill was never forgotten.

When I was a little boy my father would pick a load of apples, about fifty wooden boxes, each weighing forty pounds, and take them to what was called the early market in Portland. The hauling was done at first with horses and wagons, but within a few years a truck was used. Many times I rode in the back of the wagon to and from Portland, a jaunt of about fifteen miles, with my feet dangling over the end of the wagon, a straw hat on my head and my dog beside me. The early market was located in a building as big as a city block and farmers would come in with their crops of vegetables, fruit and berries, and sell to the grocery owners directly off their wagons and trucks. The market opened at midnight and would close around eight o'clock in the morning. A market master charged each farmer a fee for selling at the market.

Going to the market with my father was fun for me. I enjoyed watching the sales and meeting other youngsters who came to market with their fathers. After the market closed, we went to a restaurant and ate breakfast. This was really a big treat. Seldom did we ever have to take any of our apples or cherries back home. Fred Meyer, who started a gigantic chain of grocery stores in the Northwest, was a regular customer buying to supply his first store. One particular morning, a Chinese merchant came to our truck and purchased eight boxes of apples. He loaded four boxes on a two-wheel hand truck and said he would come back for the other four at which time he would pay us. He wheeled the four boxes away and then never came back. On the way home I told my father we certainly got gypped because the fellow never came back. My father was philosophical about it, saying that if he cheated us intentionally he would some day not feel good about it, but he pointed out that possibly there was a good reason why he did not return. This bothered me, but I soon forgot the incident until about a month later when another Chinese gentleman came to our truck. He questioned my father if he ever sold apples to one of his countrymen and was not paid for the purchase. My father said this was true, and the gentleman asked him how many boxes were involved. My father told him four, and the gentleman said, "You are the one." He paid my father for the four boxes and explained that when his friend was loading the apples on his truck outside the market he had suffered a heart attack and had been immediately taken to the hospital. Before his friend died, he had to promise to find us and pay for the apples. I was impressed with this honesty and, to this day, I have a warm spot for the Chinese people.

When my father was ninety-two, he was called for jury duty. At this age, his memory was very poor. He was so excited about being asked to serve that he told my sister he intended to buy a new suit. My sister called the court and informed the clerk of my father's age and described his poor memory. They, of course, excused him which really disappointed him. We didn't dare tell him about my sister's call to the court clerk.

Father was quite the patriot, and when we were little we were taught to stand at attention and salute the flag as it went by. From the time my father came to this country and became eligible to vote, until he died, he never failed to vote. Sometimes, he walked in the rain for a mile and a half just to cast his vote. At the time he was in the hospital over the well water incident, he requested a mail-in ballot. He often reminded us that many people in Europe did not have an opportunity to vote and impressed upon us that voting is a rare privilege.

My father's memory faded considerably toward the end of his life. I recall one night I stopped at the house while he was having supper that my sister had prepared for him. In the middle of the meal he got up and put on his jacket. My sister asked him where he was going, and he said that he was going out to feed Chub and Dutch—the two horses from sixty years ago. My sister told him that we no longer had the horses and that we now had tractors. This did not satisfy him and he continued to dress to go outside to feed the horses. I then spoke up and told him that I had just fed the horses. This satisfied him and he sat down again to dinner. He said, "Lou, you are a good boy." I was over fifty years old at that time, but my father still thought of me as a young boy.

A few weeks before his death at age ninety-two, my father was taken to the hospital. The doctor suggested that after a two-week stay that he be placed in a convalescent home for a few weeks to receive proper care and medication until we could take him back home. I visited him the first night at the convalescent home, and it was apparent that he was very unhappy. I assured him that his stay would only be temporary—for a week or two—and then he would be home again.

His final comment as I was leaving his room was, "I am going to get out of this place one way or another." Early the next morning we received a telephone call that he had died. True to his word, his adventurous spirit and great sense of independence would not permit him to be contained.

My father's death was reported in the December 1976 issue of *The Gardener* magazine:

Joseph Ruchek

The Portland Garden Club has lost a good friend with the recent death of Joseph Ruchek. He was an orchardist from Beaverton who planted Lady Apple trees in that area. It was his fruit we have sold for so many years at the Market Basket. He also made the very attractive wooden apple boxes.

Mr. Ruchek was born in Czechoslovakia in 1884. He was twelve years old when apprenticed to a cooper. At the age of seventeen he came to America and landed in Beaverton, Oregon, on an old farm. He made barrels for the maraschino cherries that were harvested in Salem. The barrels were of a special nature and had to be soaked in brine.

On his farm was a Lady Apple tree planted by a pioneer and brought all the way from Louisiana. It was from this start that he developed his apple orchard. Mr. Ruchek was a farmer from the old school. Nothing was impossible. If he needed a grading or washing machine he made it. If his orchard needing tilling or ditching, he did the work by hand.

Joseph Ruchek's interest in the Portland Garden Club (he really enjoyed supplying us with Lady Apples) will truly be long remembered and Mr. Ruchek will be missed by us all.

My father was like the great majority of immigrants who came to this country seeking a new life and an opportunity to work hard and be successful. They contributed greatly to this country with their strong work ethics, their honesty, love of country and their common sense.

LOUIS J. RUCHEK
MY CHILDHOOD YEARS

I was born on June 20, 1920, on the farm my father owned in Beaverton, Oregon. Dr. Mason, the country doctor, assisted in bringing me into this world. After many years of taking care of patients, a school on my father's property was named after him. Beaverton had two doctors at this time. Both were honorable men. Even during the Depression, money wasn't their main consideration—the treatment of patients was their number one priority. Unlike today, the treatments usually took place at the patient's home.

When I was about two years old, my mother and father took me to the field where they were working. It wasn't uncommon for parents to care for young children and work in the field at the same time. That particular day, my father was plowing with our two huge grays, Dutch and Chub, when both horses came to a quick stop. My father tried to urge them on, slapping their behinds with the leather reins to make them move forward. Chub was willing to move, but Dutch stood her ground and refused to go on. After my father's numerous attempts to make Dutch move ahead failed, he came around in front of the horses to see why Dutch was being so contrary. As it turned out, I was in the furrow just a few feet away from Dutch's front hooves. There was absolutely no way this massive draft horse could have moved forward without stepping on me. That was why Dutch was determined not to move, no matter how much my father urged her. Needless to say, Dutch received an extra pail of oats that night.

I found out at a very young age that small boys and yellow jacket nests don't mix. I was playing near a yellow jacket nest and one of the yellow jackets crawled underneath my pant leg and stung me, "You know where." My father happened to be looking and saw me jump three feet straight up in the air. I barely recall him rushing me to the creek and placing mud on the wounded area to give me relief. I never had much use for yellow jackets after that and should have learned to give them plenty of space. But, I didn't.

When I was about five years old, my sister, brother and I were walking from Beaverton to our home. Houses were clustered in the center of the city for two or three blocks and then they were spaced out to about one house every half mile. The population of Beaverton in 1925 was about 800. Today there are 80,000 residents and the entire area is built up with stores, shopping centers and apartment houses.

We were walking on 117th, then a dirt lane road with brush on each side. About one-half mile from the center of Beaverton, we spotted a big yellow jacket nest on one of the branches of a brush tree. The hive, white and gray in color, was as large as a basketball. I was fascinated by it and, remembering how I had been stung once before, I wanted to throw something at the hive. As soon as I picked up a clod of dirt, my brother and sister yelled at me, "Don't you dare." Knowing that I had a mind of my own, they were already starting to run. I threw the dirt clod, striking the nest right smack in the middle. I was amazed to see how many angry yellow jackets poured out of that hive— stingers intact and hungry for victims. I just stood there like a statue as the bees flew over my head towards my sister and brother who, fortunately, were fast runners and already quite a distance from the hive. They were only stung once or twice, but I didn't get any dinner that evening. What I did get, was a stern lecture from my parents to listen to my older sister and brother. I was fortunate to escape a spanking but, all in all, and as small as I was, it felt good to get back at the yellow jackets for what they had done to me years before.

When I was four or five years old, my father, at apple harvest time, sold his apples to Bradley Pies in Portland, Oregon. Beaverton is located about seven miles from Portland and we delivered the apples using Dutch and Chub to pull a wagon loaded with fifty forty-pound boxes of apples. My dog and I enjoyed sitting on the edge of the back of the wagon on the all day trip. The man in charge of the pie factory would always come out and talk to us. He took a liking to me and, on one occasion, he gave me several pies to take home. He also gave me a knife so I would be able to sample a piece of pie on the way home. My problem then became one of choosing which pie to try. Well, how would you expect a five-year-old to solve such a problem? I did the best I could, and tried a piece of each. There were several different kinds of berry pies, along with banana and chocolate. By the time we got home, I was one very sick little boy. I learned a valuable lesson about eating habits at an early age.

The trip from the farm in Beaverton to Portland by horse and wagon was very slow. There were only a few houses in the woods on each side of the road. Now the area is totally filled with homes, business establishments and apartments, and the old, narrow, two-lane paved road is now a six-lane freeway.

There is a hill and an area between Portland and Beaverton called Sylvan. On top of the hill there was a feed store operated by a nice man by the name of Kelly. Mr. Kelly delivered hay to us and every time he came to the farm he always had a bag of candy for my sister, brother and me. He was a bachelor and owned about 500 acres of land in the valley west of Beaverton. Mr. Kelly willed this land to the Catholic Church and, even today, it is still undeveloped.

One night, a robber entered Mr. Kelly's feed store. Unfortunately, Mr. Kelly was shot and killed when he attempted to take the gun away from the thief. The case was never solved and thirty years after the murder the police took it off their files. Mr. Kelly's murder was the talk of the town for some time. People were quite disturbed that such a horrible crime had been committed in their community.

When I was seven years old, it was my job to milk Daisy, our black and white Holstein milk cow, every morning and night. It was a tiresome and somewhat boring job for a seven-year-old, but I amused myself by seeing if I could hit our cat's mouth with a stream of milk as she sat on the barn floor near me. This became a daily ritual and the cat, Mandy, would immediately sit down as soon as I was ready to milk Daisy. I got to be a pretty good shot and Mandy had a great treat twice a day.

There was always a great deal of work on the farm and my sister, brother and I were expected to help as much as we could. I was working in the fields, mostly hoeing vegetables, at the age of seven or eight. Every night my mother would order me to take a bath in a metal tub. I was not all that receptive to taking a bath, particularly if the room was cold. And what a chore it was to take a bath in those days. First you had to heat the water on the stove and then carry it to the tub. Besides, I just couldn't see why it was so necessary to wash away a "little" dirt every single night. After all, I was just going to work in the field and get dirty all over again the next day. When I was about nine, my father built a new house with a regular bathtub and hot and cold running water. It was much nicer and a lot less work to take a bath but, as hard as I tried, I still couldn't convince my mother that I didn't need one every night.

When I was five or six years old my father sold his apples right on the farm property. Mr. Fendal owned Western Fruit Company in Portland. The first time he came to the farm with his truck on a Sunday to buy some of our apples there was quite an argument over the price—my father started high and Mr. Fendal started low. Around and around they went until they finally compromised on a price. After all the haggling was done, I recall Mr. Fendal saying he would pay the price but he would never come to our farm again to buy apples. I was really worried so after he left I asked my father who was going to buy our apples. My father told me, "Don't worry. He'll be back." Sure enough, Mr. Fendal came again and again, and each time the two men would go through the same routine of haggling over the price of the apples. I finally decided that they actually enjoyed all that sparring.

Once, when I was alone with Mr. Fendal, he reached in his pocket and started to hand me a quarter. I thanked him, but told him I could not accept it because my parents had taught me to work for money. Mr. Fendal seemed quite amused at this and said this created quite a problem. After pausing a brief moment he said, "Do you see that mud puddle over there? Now, what if I dropped the quarter in the puddle? You would have to work to get it out and then you could keep the quarter. Would you do that?" I told him that didn't seem like work to me and I was sorry, but I still could not take his quarter. He then said, "Well, after you take the quarter out of the mud puddle you will have to work very hard washing your hands and cleaning up— won't you?" Now, this additional explanation made a lot of sense to me and I fished the quarter out of the puddle after he left.

Mr. Fendal finally sold his fruit company and during his retirement he would occasionally come out to the farm to visit us. He proved to be a wonderful friend to our family and I was quite fond of him.

I attended Beaverton Grade School, about a mile and a half from our farm. There was only one way to get to and from school—walk. I walked a lot of miles going to grade school and high school. In those days, we didn't need to take a physical education class. Those brisk walks to and from school, especially in cold and rainy weather, provided us a lot of exercise.

I had a cocker spaniel named "Whizzer." (All I will say is that he was aptly named as a pup.) Every day, Whizzer walked about a half a mile with me on my way to school, and then I would order him to go home. It required several commands but, eventually, he reluctantly obeyed and left me to go on by myself.

When I was in the first or second grade, I threw a piece of wadded paper at one of the girls in class. Unfortunately, the teacher happened to be looking and the girl let out a sharp yelp on top of that. There were about forty students in the class and I was called to the front. The teacher instructed me to pull my pant legs up to my knees and she used a good-sized ruler to spank the calves of my legs. The pain was insignificant compared to the embarrassment I suffered. It certainly taught me that I could not get away with anything at school. There were consequences for every deed. Furthermore, I was aware that if my parents found out there would be additional punishment at home. I made my sister promise that she would not tell them what had happened at school.

I loved books as a child. I always took a book home from the library, especially when the weather was cold. I must have read "Mutiny On The Bounty" at least three times.

I remember a lot of snow in the winter. One winter, I was walking home from second grade and the snow had piled up to the top of the fence, allowing me to walk over the top of the fence. I didn't mind taking care of the farm's animals in the winter. It gave me a snug feeling knowing they were in the barn where it was warm and dry, and they had plenty to eat.

I learned at an early age that crime does not pay. When I was about seven years old, I walked to school with two boys who were several years older than I. Their nicknames were Dummy and Zig. We would walk along the main street of Beaverton on our way to school. At that time, Beaverton consisted of about a block of businesses and houses, including a hardware store, a tavern, a bus stop, a restaurant and a post office. The mayor's house was located in the middle of town right across from the bus stop. He was a teacher at the grade school and in the summer he raised garlic and pickles next to our acreage. Later, he became a state senator and helped pass a bill to permit dog racing in Oregon.

George's grocery store was located on the main street in the middle of town. One afternoon after school, Zig, Dummy and I were walking home. As usual, we passed in front of George's store. We noticed that George had placed a table on the sidewalk and, on that table, were lots of coconuts stacked in a pyramid about two feet high. We passed the table twice and talked about how good it would be to crack one of the coconuts and eat the inside. On the way home, we continued to talk about how good the coconut would be and how we could get one.

We didn't have the money to buy one, so we went to my tree house to discuss the matter. We could only come up with one answer: steal one. Now, this was during the time of Al Capone and we thought that every successful robbery had to be well planned. So, the three of us sat there and took great pains to plan the "Great Brink's Coconut Robbery."

We finally decided that Dummy would walk by the coconuts, I would be in the middle and Zig would be to my right. Dummy was supposed to take a coconut from the table and slip it underneath his jacket. Zig and I were the lookouts and would check forward and to the rear when Dummy made the big swipe.

I recall feeling very uncomfortable about the whole idea that night when I went to bed. I didn't really want to do it, but I didn't want to chicken out either. The next day, we approached the coconut table and, after telling Dummy the coast was clear, he made his move. However, instead of taking the top coconut from the pyramid pile, Dummy (most appropriately named) grabbed one from the middle of the stack.

This, of course, disturbed the other coconuts and they all tumbled down—falling on the sidewalk and rolling into the street underneath the passing cars. Chaos reigned! George came charging out from inside his store. Dummy and Zig were already running away. What about me, you ask? Well, I was amazed at the turn of events and simply stood there looking at all those rolling coconuts. I knew I was in deep trouble, particularly after George asked me if we were stealing his coconuts. I told him the truth and said if he would let me go and not tell my folks that I would never steal anything again for the rest of my life. George passed away quite some time ago but, if he is looking down at me now, he could say that I really kept my word. Looking back, I suspect George told my father about the incident, but made him promise not to discipline me. I believe George took pity on me because I was the youngest and because I didn't run away like the other two boys.

When I was about nine years old I was not considered bashful. On the contrary, I got along with everybody and was quite inquisitive. That's what landed me in more trouble.

I was walking home from grade school when I heard a lot of activity inside of the shop area of Pete's Garage. I went to investigate and I saw two mechanics and two salesmen shooting dice and yelling loudly. This was taking place during the Depression and the nickels, dimes and quarters they were gambling with were considered "big" money. I had only watched the game for a few minutes when one of the players, as a joke, asked me if I wanted to get in. They were all laughing, and to stop their laughter I fished out the only dime I had in my pocket and threw it out in the playing area on the concrete floor. They told me to throw the dice and, believe it or not, I made ten straight passes. I was going to make my eleventh throw when I realized that all of them were broke. I had won a total of $17 and some cents. I suggested I give them their money back but they refused, saying I won it fair and square and that it was worth it to see someone make ten straight passes. When I walked away with my winnings tucked into my overalls I limped on one side because the coins were that heavy. I was elated until I thought of something that dampened my spirit—what if my parents found out that I had gambled? What to do? What to do? If I kept the money in my room or in the house there was a good chance my mother would find my newly acquired wealth. It helped a little that the men at the garage had promised me they would not tell anyone about my winnings. Now, $17 was a huge amount of money and, finally, I decided the best way to handle the situation was to take one of my mother's fruit jars, wrap up the coins in cloth and bury the jar at a fence post. Whenever I needed some extra money I would go out at night, dig up the jar and take what I needed.

Everything was going along just fine until I made a fatal mistake. I was walking to school one morning with five of my friends when we stopped at the Beaverton Bakery. As usual, we looked through the window at all the fresh doughnuts and rolls that we could not afford to buy. However, because there was plenty of money in my money well, I volunteered to buy each of my friends a doughnut or two. I ended up buying a couple dozen doughnuts for about thirty cents. I passed the doughnuts around and we even had some left over to eat on the way home from school. These were my friends and I had no qualms repaying them for favors they had done for me in the past.

Lightening struck when I got home that night. It happened that after my purchase of the doughnuts, my mother stopped in the bakery and purchased a few doughnuts too. The lady at the counter knew us, and she made a remark about how our family must really like doughnuts. Of course, it all came out when I got home that evening and I had to explain

how I was able to afford to buy the doughnuts. Again, I was
lucky I didn't get a spanking, but I had to promise my father I wouldn't do any more gambling until I was twenty-
one. Also, his first inclination was for me to return the money
that was left, but then he said he thought the men deserved
to lose it for getting me into the game in the first place.
Later there was some talk around our small town that someone had made ten straight passes with the dice and it caused
many a good argument.

When I was about eighteen, a friend of mine wanted me
to go to the dog races. I went to my father and told him I
would like to break my promise about gambling to go to the
races. He objected at first, but relented when I asked him to
explain the difference between his losing $5,000 in Philco
stock when they went broke and my betting a few dollars on
the dogs. To this day I think of the Beaverton Bakery and the
dice game whenever I see a doughnut. Later on, I rarely
gambled except for a little penny ante poker once in awhile
while I was in the service, and one other time when I spent
some time at a poker table in Reno while I was investigating
an airport case.

Why did I buy as many doughnuts as I did—only to
give them away? I did it because it was a time of deprivation.
It was a time when people demonstrated firsthand the spirit
of helping, giving and sharing with others. I was taught to
share. My mother, bless her, was probably one of the most
giving people I've ever known. I remember her bringing hot
coffee and cake to the WPA workers. These people were total strangers to us and cleaned our creek in the cold and rainy
weather. It was not uncommon for people to help one another
during the Depression. I remember my father and Mr. Bernard, a man who later owned an airport, drove to a grain mill
in Newberg. They brought sacks of their own wheat to be
ground into flour. They also took some sacks of wheat from
other neighbors so they too could have flour to make bread.
Today, the remaining members of the Bernard family own

the Beaverton Shopping Center, one of the largest shopping centers in the state. Their shopping center is located on the property that once was the airport. The Bernard family is a good example of good things happening to people who do good things for others.

Center Street, which bordered the south side of our farm, is now a three-lane thoroughfare, but when I was young, it was a narrow muddy road in the winter with deep potholes. In the summer, it was a gravel road that threw up huge dust clouds whenever a car traveled on it. In order for two vehicles to pass, the drivers had to use the dirt shoulders.

About a mile to the west of our farm, a young man owned a wrecking lot. He was a fantastic mechanic and he and my father built a concrete mixer during the Depression. The mixer consisted of a two-horse gasoline engine that churned an iron barrel. This mechanic always had older cars around, and in the summer showed up in a Willy's Knight convertible. He had the Willy's wide open and, at times, we could see him coming a half a mile away on Center Street because of the dust cloud he created. On several occasions he roared into my mother's chickens on the road and, more than once, killed one or two. He would then stop, pay my mother for the chickens and stay to enjoy a chicken dinner that night. Funny, my mother never objected.

I was about ten when there was an incident by our farm on Center Street. It was around two o'clock in the morning when my father and I were awakened by loud knocking on our kitchen door. We looked out the door's window and saw two of the toughest looking individuals you would ever want to see. My father asked them what they wanted. One of them spoke up and said that their truck was stuck in a mud hole on Center Street, and asked if we had anything that could pull their truck out of the mud. My father and I went to the barn and harnessed Dutch and Chub, our powerful draft horses that could pull an apartment building off its foundation. We went with the horses to a big yellow truck with its rear wheels buried up to the axle in mud. We hooked a chain to the front bumper and Dutch and Chub easily did the rest. After the truck was out of the mud, one of the men came over to my father and gave him twenty dollars. There was a great Depression in the country and twenty dollars was a tremendous amount of money. I questioned my father as to what the truck was loaded with to make it so heavy. My father said there were sacks of sugar and bottles and that, most likely, moonshine was involved. This was during prohibition times.

My father gave me a dollar for helping him harness the horses and the following day I treated three of my friends to hamburgers and soft drinks. Hamburgers were a dime and soft drinks were a nickel. My friends were very curious how I obtained the money for the treats. I told them how our horses had pulled the heavy truck out of the mud on Center Street and how my father was given twenty dollars. To make the story more interesting, I told them that the men were moonshine racketeers, somewhat like Al Capone's friends. I further sweetened the story by telling them that I thought I saw a Thompson submachine gun in the front seat of the truck. My storytelling and treating my friends to hamburgers and soft drinks made my story all the more plausible, and I was quite the hero for some time.

The Depression was full of hard times and it wasn't uncommon for people to help their neighbors and friends. This helping hand philosophy was shared with the children.

When I was a small boy, I remember a lady wearing no shoes stopping at the farm with two little barefoot girls. They were on their way to the strawberry fields to make a little money picking berries. They had another three miles to walk and they stopped at our farmhouse to see if they could get something to eat. My mother not only fed them, but also gave some shoes to the little girls. In those days, you repaired a hole in a shoe by placing a piece of cardboard inside the shoe.

We were very fortunate during the Depression because we had shelter and good food from the farm. I can recall a lot of people stopping at the farm for something to eat. They always offered to work for what they received and I don't remember anyone ever being turned away hungry. During the Depression thirty million people were out of work with no opportunity to earn money.

In one of the Depression years, my father said we earned $100 for the year's work after expenses. He went to a stockbroker and asked him to purchase a certain bank bond. The broker told my father that he knew how hard we all had worked to earn the $100. He advised my father that he was wasting his money by buying that bond, and he would rather see him throw that money out of the window, so that at least the people down below could benefit. Instead of accepting the broker's argument that the bond was worthless, my father told him that he intended to buy this particular bond and, if he would not sell it to him, he would go elsewhere. My father purchased the bond, and later, when the economy changed, for many years the bond paid about $500 per year interest plus a generous final payout.

When I was nine, my mother sent me to the store to purchase groceries for our dinner that night. She gave me a dollar bill to buy a large amount of hamburger, bread and other groceries. With the dollar in my pocket, I walked up the lane where the yellow jacket nest had been. I neared some vacant land (now a shopping center) and noticed a group of boys my age playing football in a cow pasture. The youngsters in the neighborhood used this pasture for football and baseball games and Sunday afternoons always found someone involved in some sport in this field. Actually, the cows pastured there turned out to be quite useful as blockers. We often ran around them with the ball tucked under our arm to avoid being tackled by someone on the other team. The only drawback, of course, was the fresh "pies" that you had to dodge.

Because I had extra time on my way to the store, I stopped to join in the football game. Some time passed before I realized I had better quit playing ball and get going to the store. When I arrived at the store, I discovered that the dollar bill my mother had given me was gone. I had lost it—possibly making an end run around one of those cows. No matter, I was in a real pickle. It was late, and I knew that my mother was depending on the groceries for the family's supper. I pondered what to do. It was getting dark and I knew it would be impossible to find the dollar bill in the pasture. (I did look for it the next day, but was unable to find it.)

I finally decided to go to Mr. Rossi, one of the wealthiest men in the city and a friend of my father's. I told Mr. Rossi about my predicament and then asked him if I could borrow a dollar. He said he would loan it to me, but asked how I was going to pay him back. This was certainly a good question, as a dollar was not at all easy to come by. I finally came up with a proposal to mow his lawn, and we made an agreement that I would mow about an acre of lawn with a hand push mower for twenty-five cents per cutting. Mr. Rossi gave me the dollar and I went to George's store and purchased the groceries.

It took considerable effort to push a hand mower over the acre of grass, but after four cuttings I had finished my part of the agreement. I then talked to Mr. Rossi and told him that I had completed my part of the bargain and thanked him for helping me with my problem. He then reached into his pocket, took out a dollar bill and gave it to me. He said he could have done this to start with, but he wanted to teach me to be responsible. Later, after returning from the war, I met Mr. Rossi on the street. After we talked about my war years, he wanted to know if I wanted to borrow some money. I told him that I appreciated his kind offer, but that I really didn't need to. With a twinkle in his eye he said, "Well, I know you would be good for it, because I taught you something about values years ago." Later, he offered me a business proposition in the City of Beaverton. I did not accept. It would have been quite profitable. You just have to look back and say, "Oh, well."

I recall summers as the best of times when I was a youngster. We always dammed the creek that originated from a year-round spring that flowed out of solid rock about a quarter of a mile from our farm, and was so pure that you could drink right out of the creek. The average flow was about five feet wide and about three feet deep. We swam with beavers. Large cranes, pelicans and other birds would land near the creek to catch a small trout or a mudsucker for their dinner. Hawks were always a problem. They would swoop down on a mother hen with chicks and grab one of the chicks for dinner. There was a huge 100-foot high fir tree snag located slightly to the north of our farm in the woods, where the hawks nested at the very top.

There was considerable watercress in the creek which, much to my surprise, was eaten at restaurants. All kinds of crawfish were in the creek. Some had huge red claws and, occasionally, one claw would be missing. I always assumed it had been lost in a fight.

When I was about five, I fished in the creek for trout. My "very modern" fishing equipment consisted of a string with a safety pin for a hook. Sometimes I got tired of waiting for the fish to bite, so I would stick the pole in the ground and join my mother and father wherever they were working. One time, my father said he thought he saw my fishing pole wiggling. I ran down to the creek, looked at my pole and was shocked to see a fifteen-pound salmon on the end of the line. Young as I was, I didn't realize that my father had been to Beaverton and purchased the salmon and put it on my hook. I gave no thought that the salmon was already cleaned when I found it on my line. I recall, however, that I kept repeating at dinner how good the baked salmon was and how you had to be a "real fisherman" to catch such a big fish.

Game was plentiful around the farm. I was a small boy of six and eating breakfast during the pheasant hunting season, when a shotgun blast went through the window right over my head into a bag of rice that sat on a shelf on the wall. The rice poured out all over my head like a waterfall cascading onto rocks in a riverbed. Apparently, a pheasant had flown between the house and the fruit trees around the house. The hunter, in an anxious moment, fired and the shot missed my head by mere inches.

There were many pheasants on the farm, especially where corn had been grown. The King pheasants loved to strut around in the grass in the orchard, and deer came to feed on the apples on the ground. Sometimes they damaged the trees by eating the bark and small branches. How different it is now. Instead of seeing deer, muskrat, beaver, otter, and all the other wildlife in the area, you look at shopping centers, apartments, commercial buildings and home after home. Recently, a governmental agency pointed out that a quarter of an acre on the farm was wetland and should be preserved for "wildlife." I went to a council meeting and pointed out that they were years late—the only wildlife left in the area was the people living in the apartment buildings surrounding the quarter of an acre.

In the late thirties, a beer baron bought the land surrounding the spring. He was a very nice man and I met him one day when I was hunting with my .22 rifle. He was handling lumber from one of the piles near the place where he was building his home. I went to him and started a conversation. He wanted to know where I lived. I told him, and he put out his hand and said, "Hi neighbor. It's nice to meet you." I was impressed, and I remarked to him that he must have a lot of money to be building this kind of home. It was a castle. The finest materials were used, including solid copper nails. The castle was surrounded by several acres of lawn and flowers and below it there was a large pool of water, or small lake. The place looked like a scene of a park in a Hollywood movie. As I recall, the house cost about $30,000, which was an enormous amount of money in those days.

Almost every Sunday during the summer, parties were held around the pool and I was fortunate to be able to attend a number of them. Tables were set aside for the children with soft drinks, ice cream and candy bars. Ham sandwiches and a nearby beer truck waited for the adults. I would dress up and join a number of children who were brought to the party by friends of the host. One day, the owner told me to come over to see a champion boxer by the name of Barney Ross. He had built a ring on the lawn near the pool where Barney trained. As a young boy, I found it very exciting to watch Barney train for a fight in Portland. Later I was given two tickets to the fight.

I was fascinated by this man who told me how he went from being broke, riding the rails in boxcars in Canada and in this country, to being the wealthy owner of a large brewery.

Although we had some time for play, basically, summer days were filled with work. There was no such thing as being paid an allowance to keep your room clean or take out the garbage. You were expected to handle your assigned chores and responsibilities on the farm without complaint in exchange for a room to sleep in and food to eat. If we wanted money, we were told to go out and earn it. My classmates at high school and the fellows I ran around with all had jobs. Jack was a caddy at Portland Golf Club. He was paid ninety cents per eighteen holes, or $1.50 for carrying two bags. Don had a huge paper route. Bill worked on his father's dairy and Al worked in his father's greenhouse. My classmates, Don Short, Jack Grauer, William Denney and Al Peterkort all turned out to be highly successful in life.

I was not permitted to play football in school because it took place in the daytime and work on the farm was considered more important. In the evenings, after chores, I played basketball in the barn where I rigged up an iron barrel hoop on the wall. I loved to play baseball in the summer. I was a catcher. One day, a liquor distributing company called me and wanted to know if I would catch a game for them on a Saturday afternoon. I asked my father if I could take the afternoon off to play in the game. My father said, "Well, there's five acres of corn to hoe. If you get a big part of that done, you can play." I worked like the dickens during the week so I could play on Saturday. At dinner, after the game, the only question I remember my father asking was whether we won or lost. Compare this with Little League today where all the kids have uniforms, transportation and treats after the game. It seems so different now. As children, we were compelled to use our imagination to create our fun and entertainment, a far cry from today's television, video games and computers.

When I was working in Kansas for the railroad, I remember a neighbor boy was in Little League because of the efforts of his father. The boy was more interested in collecting butterflies. While he was playing center field in one of the games, a butterfly flew by him. He took off after the butterfly and followed it out of the ball field, leaving center field vacant. The game was stopped. Even though I'm not absolutely certain, I'd bet you a fairly good sum that that boy never played in the Major Leagues.

I graduated from Beaverton High School in 1938. At that time there was one high school for an area covering a radius of about six miles. The high school student population was about 200. At the present time, we have six high schools with enrollments of about 1500 students in each.

Our principal's name was Mike Metzler. He was a tough, but fair principal who ran a tight ship and was nicknamed Iron Mike. He was not only in charge of both the grade school and the high school, but he was in charge of the busing system, a teacher and a coach of sports. His only assistant was an elderly lady who worked in the office and served as his secretary. I remember him as a very busy man who worked long, long hours for meager pay. He attended all the school board meetings and was highly respected in the community.

Today's principals don't have the arsenal of disciplinary tools that was available to Mr. Metzler. Let me give you an example. If any student would have come to Mr. Metzler's school wearing a long black trench coat and dark glasses, he would have grabbed that student by an ear, hauled him out of the building and told him to come back properly dressed.

In addition to his administrative duties as the principal, Mr. Metzler also taught a civics class. I was half asleep in his class one warm sunny spring day when he was lecturing about issues in government. At one point, he asked the entire class to vote on a governmental issue in his lecture by a show of hands. Being half asleep, I failed to vote. Unfortunately, Mr. Metzler noticed and asked me why I didn't vote with the rest of the class. I didn't want to own up that I hadn't been paying attention and didn't even know what the vote was about so I answered the only way I could by telling him that *I wasn't old enough to vote.*

Except for Mr. Metzler, the entire class laughed and laughed—until Mr. Metzler told me I was to stay and see him after class. He waited until everyone left the classroom and then lectured me on how I should stay awake in his class. He ended the conversation, however, by admitting that he had enjoyed my answer. He also suggested that I put more effort into my schoolwork. I was ever alert in his class after that and we enjoyed many good political arguments.

I was proud to be a member of my high school's debate team that went to the district finals.

The teachers in those days were mostly elderly unmarried women who showed tremendous interest in their students. It seemed that the children they taught became their extended family because they didn't have children of their own.

Miss Sanford, a teacher, was in charge of senior plays. We were sure "Discipline" was her middle name, but here again, she was very fair and helpful. One day, she approached me to be in the senior play. I told her that I wasn't too interested, but she had this twinkle in her eye and said she was sure that I would change my mind when I heard about the part she had in mind for me. She then explained that I would play the part of a long lost husband who comes home at the very end of the play as the curtain comes down and, without saying a word, enters center stage and kisses the leading lady. I didn't have a single line to say. I just had to come out on the stage and kiss the leading girl. Now, the leading girl was very pretty and I only had to think about Ms. Sanford's proposal for a brief moment before deciding that it might be in my best interest to be more cooperative and agree to assist in the program. Needless to say, I enjoyed my part in the senior play because there were several rehearsals.

Teachers like Ms. Sanford were dedicated to their students. A female teacher was always neatly dressed and a male teacher always wore a suit and tie. Students always addressed teachers as Mr., Mrs. or Miss. Teachers not only taught the basic subjects, but they also stressed the importance of honesty, perseverance and the value of a strong work ethic.

We did not get away with anything. For example, Miss Sanford told two male students they were to take a make-up test the next day and strongly suggested they study for the test that night. The following day, the two students went to Miss Sanford and told her that they had had a flat tire the night before and needed another night to study for the make-up test. They explained how the flat tire incident had kept them from "hitting the books." Of course, this simply was not true as they had both been goofing off. Miss Sanford granted the two boys the additional night to study and the following day the boys were given their test. She separated the two in different rooms and instructed them to answer all of the questions in writing. They did just fine on the test until they ran into the last question—"Which tire on the car went flat?" The boys knew they had been outsmarted which ended the matter.

Years later, when I was working as an investigator for the railroad and riding trains in the east, I often thought of the wonderful teachers I had in school, and how much I owed them, for it was their kindness and guidance that helped mold my life.

A LIFE OF MY OWN

After I graduated from high school my father and I had a long talk. He pointed out that I could go to college, however, I would have to work myself through—that he would help a little, but there were no free rides. He felt that a person would appreciate college more if he had to work and pay for it himself. I told him that I planned to get a job and go to college later. My father said that I could get my own living quarters, or I could live with the family. However, if I chose to live with the family, I would have to pay room and board to my mother. It wasn't that my father did not want to help me, but he was convinced it was time for me to stand on my own two feet. He counseled me that it was a tough world out there and a boy had to prepare for it. If he didn't, he would have a miserable later life. I did not fully appreciate what my father was telling me at the time. But, looking back, I realize he was trying his best to give me the tools I needed to become self-sufficient.

I chose to live at home while I worked. I paid my mother money for room and board and for doing my laundry. My wonderful mother saved all the money I paid her and when I got married she gave all of it back to me as one of her wedding gifts. It wasn't uncommon to feel that children should earn their own way as soon as they graduated from high school. Years later, when I worked as an investigator for the railroad, I was often amazed to see sons and daughters in their thirties still living at home with their parents for free, or living in homes that their parents had purchased for them.

In 1938, I went out into the world and felt lucky to find work at the Peterkort Greenhouses. The pay was a whopping twenty cents per hour. Mr. Peterkort's sons and I had gone to school and played basketball together.

Mr. Peterkort was another immigrant who came to this country with very little money. Yet, even though times were hard, he established a thriving greenhouse business.

There were four of us young fellows working at the greenhouses. In the summertime it was necessary to change the dirt in the wooden benches that measured about a foot deep, four feet wide and 400 feet long. We would strip down to our waists, shovel the dirt from the bench to a wheelbarrow, wheel the old dirt out and wheel the new dirt in. It was hard labor and the inside of those glass greenhouses was very hot. It wasn't uncommon for Mr. Peterkort to come to the greenhouse where we had been digging and wheeling dirt all day long at just about quitting time. He would look over what we had accomplished during the day and say in a joking way, "Well, you didn't do all that much today, but we will give it hell tomorrow." This, of course, was not too inspiring, but it was also his way of saying we had done a good day's work.

I also got to work with all kinds of flowers—everything from chrysanthemums to ferns and, although I enjoyed the work, I knew that I wasn't interested in making a career of raising flowers. I didn't have the money to go to college, so I decided to go to business college at night and take accounting and typing. I could still work all day and study or attend school at night. I became friendly with another student at the college and when we were trying to decide what additional class to take, I suggested we take Gregg Shorthand. I thought it would be unique to be able to take down conversations and told him it would be like learning a new language. Honestly, he wasn't too crazy about the idea because, at that time, shorthand was more or less considered a girl's subject. After a lot of discussion, I was able to convince him to take the course. The fact that we were the only two boys in a class of thirty girls made it very interesting. We never had a shortage of volunteers to help us study for tests and we never had a shortage of dates. Afterwards, my friend could never thank me enough for convincing him to take the class.

It was about this time that I purchased a 1938 Chevrolet. Unfortunately, the first day I had the car I was cruising Broadway in Portland with some of my friends when one of them said, "Hey, look at that pretty blond with that man on the corner." Of course, I looked and took my eyes off what was in front of me. The next thing I knew, I had rear-ended the car in front of me. The driver of the other car was an older gentleman who commented that he too had been looking at the blonde and could understand the lack of attention to my driving.

INTRODUCTION TO
UNION PACIFIC RAILROAD

After attending night school for about a year, I resigned my job at the greenhouse and went to school full time until I graduated. I could type 95 words a minute and was able to take shorthand at 150 words a minute. This was 1940 and there just weren't any jobs around of any consequence. Finally, a friend of mine told me that Union Pacific Railroad was looking for a male stenographer. At that time, the upper brass on the railroad had private cars and each had a male stenographer as his secretary. Women were not permitted to work on the private cars because the officials of the railroad lived in the cars—sometimes for weeks at a time.

The day after I heard about the job, I applied. A gentleman by the name of Mr. Ashley was conducting the interviews. There were about twenty applicants applying for the one job. After I sat down, Mr. Ashley reviewed my brochure. I could tell that, for some reason, he was not interested in giving me a shorthand or a typing test. I then spoke up and said, "Mr. Ashley, I know what you are going to do with my brochure." He asked me to please tell him what he was going to do with it. I told him that he was going to file my brochure in the dead files or in the wastepaper basket. I then told him that I really needed the job, that I had checked on Union Pacific and that they were an excellent company to work for. I told him that I was young and I would work for them for a long time—that this would be a good union for both sides if he hired me. After I finished my little speech, Mr. Ashley had a change of attitude and told me to come in the next morning to take the tests. I passed those tests and I worked for Union Pacific Railroad for forty years, retiring in 1980. I enjoyed all my years working for the railroad and they remain a good company to work for to this very day.

Toward the end of my career with the railroad I had business in Washington, D.C. with Oregon Senator, Mark Hatfield. I found Senator Hatfield to be congenial, helpful and down to earth. After our business was concluded, he asked how I had started working for Union Pacific Railroad. He said he was curious because his father had been an employee of the Southern Pacific Railroad for many years. He said he was aware how difficult it was to get a job on the railroad in the early years. When I told him about my conversation with Mr. Ashley, Senator Hatfield asked me if Mr. Ashley was still living. I told him that he was not and the senator said, "He must be looking down at you now and saying that young fellow was sincere when he said he would work for the railroad for a long time, and that it would be a good union."

Later, when I was in charge of claims investigations of the Northwest Division for the railroad I interviewed prospective claims investigators. One applicant's brochure indicated he had graduated from the University of Oregon, but the year after he graduated was blank. I asked him what he had done during that year. He told me that he had taken a year off and traveled all over the United States and Canada. I asked him if the travel bug was pretty much out of his system and he answered, "Possibly." I admired his honesty, but I was not about to take a year or two to train an investigator and then have him decide to take a year off to travel.

Prior to the war, I first went to work as a secretary for the Chief Engineer of Buildings and Tracks for the entire Northwest District. I learned a great deal about what it took to keep the railroad running and on the tracks.

Later, I was transferred to LaGrande where I was secretary to the Chief Dispatcher. At LaGrande I learned about the nuts and bolts operation of the railroad. It was a good place to learn because, at that time, LaGrande was a terminal point and had a repair yard. The yard contained extra steam helper engines to assist the heavy freight trains over the nearby mountain hump areas. The Chief Dispatcher was in his late seventies and his knowledge of railroading seemed unlimited. At the beginning, he was a little reserved with me, but a friendship developed and he would even let me off for a few days when my sister came to visit.

I had been in LaGrande for about six months when a position opened up in the accounting department in Portland. With my schooling in accounting, I took the job and started work calculating trainmen's time and pay on various runs. I was saving a considerable amount of my $150 monthly salary and, after just a few months, I purchased a 1937 Sport Ford V-8 Coupe. On my days off, when I was not helping on the farm, I would give my car two or three coats of wax in a single day. What a beauty!

IN THE NAVY

The date was December 7, 1941, and I was on my way to a gas station when the news came over my car radio that the Japanese had attacked Pearl Harbor. The following day, I enlisted in the U.S. Navy and by Christmas of 1941 I was in boot camp in San Diego. Throughout my naval career I was known, as many were, as a "Pearl Harbor Recruit."

I didn't have any problems in boot camp except for bayonet practices. During one particular practice, my competitor partner was an ex-army man who was quite skilled in using the bayonet. Several times he came dangerously close to my body with bayonet lunges. I finally had to tell him to, "Take it easy. I'm not the enemy." Even though he apologized and said that he was aware that at times he got carried away, I never really did feel too comfortable as we continued the practice.

One time, a bunch of us went to town on liberty. There was a southern boy from Alabama who told us that his father was in the moonshine business. It was evident that he liked his hard liquor. Before returning to the base, he stopped at a liquor store and purchased a pint of whiskey. He then made a bet with us that he could bring the whiskey into the barracks past the guard at the gate. Now, we all knew that the Marine guards were thorough and a number of us took the bet. When we were about a half a block from the Marine sentry, the southern boy drank the entire bottle of whiskey at one time. He then proceeded through the gate by the sentry guard without any problem. After walking about a half a block from the gate, the alcohol hit him and he was quite inebriated. He was not intoxicated enough, however, to forget that we all owed him money. Years later, when I was working as an investigator, a time element was an essential point where liquor was consumed just before an accident. While in boot camp, one day I had the duty of serving the sailors their food in the mess hall. It was my job to use a large ladle to dish out a heavy, reddish-yellow and lumpy squash sauce from a huge aluminum container onto the trays of the men as they passed by in line. That was, of course, if they asked for it. Another server who was about five feet down the line from me was serving green beans. Prior to mealtime we made a bet that I would out-do him by serving more of my squash concoction than he would green beans. This wasn't too smart of a bet on my part. The line of sailor recruits started to pass through and after I called out "squash" they would immediately turn up their noses and pass me by to accept the green beans. I was losing my bet big time and decided I needed to take drastic action. When the sailors asked what was in my serving container I would call out "sweet potatoes." Surprisingly, it seemed everyone wanted "sweet potatoes." On a number of occasions I would give them two heaping ladles of "sweet potatoes"—even if they looked like they really only wanted one. I won my bet, but my conscience started to bother me so I told the green bean server what I had done. We called off the bet and I saved money because I didn't have to pay for losing. He then joined in the fun by asking the sailors who did not take sweet potatoes if they were certain they didn't want to go back and get some before it was too late and they were all gone. Some came back and I talked them into receiving two ladles on their trays. We had a barrel of fun that day. That whole day there was only one sailor who came back and questioned the "mistake" I made in calling out "sweet potatoes." He came up after he had eaten his lunch and told me that the "sweet potatoes" were certainly not as good as the ones that were grown in the southern states. With tongue-in-cheek (after all, what could I say) I told him it could probably be attributed to the soil or that the southerners were better farmers. He also said it would have been better served baked in a sort of "squash" fashion. I agreed with him and told him I would pass his excellent suggestion on to the cooks. After we finished lunch the cooks stopped by and gave themselves quite a pat on the back remarking that they thought their squash sauce went exceedingly well. They further advised they intended to put it back on the menu in the very near future. Fortunately, I did not have to do any more serving of food in my Navy career. Actually, the food in the Navy was exceptional—even in a battle zone.

In my later life I nearly had another "sweet potato" run-in. I interviewed a witness in a murder case and he invited me to stay for dinner. He said they were having possum and sweet potatoes. Now, I had to "play possum" on that one. I told him I was crestfallen but, in view of very important appointments scheduled for that same night, I just could not accept his kind dinner invitation.

Can you see me? I am the one smiling in the 16th row. (1941)

My friends and me. I am on the far left. (1942)

After boot camp, I was assigned to a flight school at Sandpoint Naval Air Station in Seattle, Washington. I was training to be a gunner-radioman on torpedo planes. However, there was a shortage of signalmen on minesweepers and I was assigned to one because I had learned to use blinker lights, flag hoists and radio and semaphore signaling in signal school. The ship I was assigned to was made out of wood, was about 150 feet long and had a crew of thirty-five men—each man a specialist. We had one electrician on board. If something went wrong electrically, it was up to him to correct the problem. In addition to my signaling duties, I was the helmsman in bad storms and when the ship was tying up or leaving the dock.

In the early part of 1942, prior to the time our minesweeper was commissioned, I was watching a civilian shipyard welder weld signal equipment on the bridge for me. I was so foolish! By that night my eyes started to burn so bad I had to go to sick bay for treatment of "welder's flash." I felt like I had sand in my eyes and it wasn't until the next morning that I recovered.

On that same day a new Filipino cook came on board. He was also a waiter for the officers. When an officer ordered him to do something, instead of saying, "Yes, Sir," he would say, "Okay." One officer patiently went into great detail explaining how to respond with, "Yes, Sir," instead of, "Okay." Finished with his lesson, he asked the cook if he understood what he said. The cook quickly replied, "Okay, I understand." After that we nicknamed him "Okay." Okay was very much a favorite with us as he was always concerned that we had plenty of coffee and sandwiches when we came off from the cold watches.

We had a very sharp crew and no matter how many years pass I will always remember them for their friendship and their companionship.

Once I was at the helm for six hours. We were in the midst of a huge storm and we all had to wear our life jackets. Visibility at times would be less than fifty feet and with the wind chill factor the temperature dropped to 20 below. About ten members of the crew were in the pilot-house with the officers. Our ship was designed to roll on its side up to 45 degrees after which it would roll completely over. Everyone's eyes were glued to the meter's needlepoint as it read 42—43—41 over and over again. The storm that night whipped up 50-foot high waves and the trick was to keep the bow straight into the waves after which we would come down like a runaway elevator. At the end of the plunge the fantail would swing and the ship had to be righted again to meet the next wave. We were all aware that an entire crew had been lost when our sister ship had recently rolled over in a storm at Coos Bay, Oregon. Needless to say, we were very thankful that we were able to withstand the storm in one piece. We learned that life was precious.

After another vicious storm our ship ended up on the beach carried there by a huge wave. That turned out to be quite a photo opportunity.

Before I was in the Navy, I thought the only reason some men joined was because they were not able to get a job on the outside. How wrong I was! These men were very talented—especially the career sailors. I saw a nineteen-year-old gunner's mate take a five-inch gun apart in what seemed like a zillion pieces and put it back perfectly.

One day an admiral came aboard to inspect our ship. During inspection of the men he walked along the line and when he came to me I brought my rifle up and threw the chamber open. He looked into the chamber and then slammed the gun back in my hands saying the word, "Clean." He was pleased with the appearance of our ship and said that he had never seen a "neater" looking one. Our ship was noted for breaking records for getting underway and for maneuvers such as picking up sweep gear.

At night, after a full day of sweeping mine fields, we all gathered around the kitchen galley table to drink coffee and swap stories. The men liked a certain story I told them about something that happened in Bremerton. I was on signal watch when Lana Turner came to the Navy yard to visit the men. As she passed by in a launch, I blinked out a message at her boat. The message was, "Welcome to Bremerton, pretty lady." I didn't think anyone could read my message and was quite surprised when she turned around and blew me a kiss. After telling my shipmates this story, they jokingly said they wanted me to teach them Morse Code.

Gunnery practice involved firing on a target that resembled a sleeve. I was assigned to the 20-millimeter gun and on the first run I fired the gun at the sleeve but instead of hitting it, one of the shells cut the towline right in front of the sleeve. The target fell into the water and the pilot had to go back and get another sleeve.

Sometimes when we were escorting tankers we stopped for short periods of time at Seward and Dutch Harbor in Alaska. We would go ashore at Seward and mix with some of the old sourdoughs. They loved to talk and had a lot of stories about panning for gold in Alaska. Another of their favorite subjects was the Kodiak bear—who weighed as much as 1,600 lbs. and measured thirteen feet in height. The old-timers told us that the Kodiak bear could move as fast as 30 mph—and could outrun a deer. One of the fellows on the ship had a brother who was a P-38 pilot. He was with a squadron that escorted bombers out of the Aleutians on their way to Japan. Because of their relationship, one brother being on our ship and the other a fighter pilot, the captain arranged a short sailing tour for about ten of the pilots. We enjoyed meeting these wonderful fellows and were always glad to see them come aboard at different times. It wasn't too long after the pilots' initial visit that we were moored to the dock and watching them perform some formation flying above the harbor. Without warning, one of the P-38's plunged downward and crashed into the harbor. I witnessed this from the top of the bridge and, yes, it was the brother of our shipmate. This was a painful jolt to all of us and it was only a short time after the fatal dive that our shipmate was transferred to the states. Our good skipper recognized that the brother of the pilot was having a difficult time, particularly at night, knowing that his brother was somewhere on the bottom of the bay. It was a sad day for all of us when he left the ship. Not long thereafter that, another one of our buddies received a telegram advising him his brother had been killed by a hitchhiker in New Orleans. To make matters worse, his brother had been supporting his mother and sister. When sad news like this came on board for a shipmate, the pain was felt by all of us. It seemed more so than in civilian life. I recall that Okay made a special pie for our shipmate after he received the bad news, and the rest of us did our best to try to keep his spirits up.

After training cruises, we left for the Aleutians where I was to spend three years aboard the minesweeper in the Bering Sea. Throughout the war, we swept for offensive and defensive mines, escorted large ships and searched for aviators who were lost going to or coming from air raids on the Japanese mainland. We chased Japanese submarines that hung around Kiska and assisted people on bases in return for supplies. We first headquartered in Dutch Harbor and, as the war progressed, we moved to Adak and then to Amchitka.

We were attacked by Japanese bombers while docked in the Amchitka harbor. In the mornings, a signalman from another ship and I would shoot the breeze using the blinker lights. He once told me that he was losing weight worrying about the daily bombings. After that I started our conversations with, "Well, how much weight have you lost since yesterday?" It was about a week later that an airfield was finished on Amchitka and the P-38's landed. Their presence ended the Japanese air raids.

Our biggest enemy was the cold, rough weather and excessive storms and winds when we were out to sea. We felt sorry for the pilots who flew from bases in the Aleutians to bomb the Japanese mainland because not only did they have the enemy to fight, but the exceptionally foul weather as well. It was amazing. The planes would take off in rather nice weather, but after ten or twenty minutes there would be a storm with 90 mph winds. These storms were called Willa-Waughs, and they came quickly and without warning. At times the ocean spray would form heavy ice, making it necessary for all hands to chip it away from the ship.

We were told that a person could only exist for about four minutes in the freezing water temperature. The winds would generate mountainous waves. I remember a particularly bad storm when every single man aboard was seasick. No matter, it was still necessary to carry on with the work if we wanted to stay afloat.

I always felt bad for the crew of mechanics in the bottom of the ship who had to tend the ship's engines. Not only did they have to contend with heavy rolling of the ship, but the men in the engine room also had to breathe the smell of diesel oil. The waves would be as high as forty feet and our ship, with a shallow draft of only nine feet to allow the hull to float over moored mines, would roll and pitch violently in rough seas.

The ship was made out of wood because wood would not attract mines like metal ships. In storms the wood would groan, creak and moan something fierce and I found myself thinking what the Mayflower passengers must have contended with when coming to America. The noise was very disturbing when we tried to sleep between watches.

I also thought the ship was made of wood to allow it to "give" when a 600 lb. mine would go off. On a number of occasions, after working exploding mines, we had to go to dry dock to secure the timbers in the hull of the ship because they had been opened when the mines exploded.

The most dangerous move when sweeping for mines was the first furrow. Once a furrow was made through a minefield, much of the danger was removed as our second and later passes would be in the lanes where we had already swept.

In clearing a minefield, we were on the lookout for three types of mines. One was the moored mine that had a chain fastened from the mine to a weight. To counter this, we had a sweep cable that would contact the mine and set it off. The next was the propeller-noise mine. These mines would go off on the sound of a ship's propeller. To destroy these mines there was a large apparatus that looked like a hammer attached to the bow of the ship. As the ship moved forward, the hammer was lowered into the water. A noise like a rivet gun inside of the hammer exploded the mines that would go off on sound. The magnetic mine, was attracted to metal-hulled ships. To set the magnetic mine off, we dragged a long, charged tail from the stern of the ship. Our ship was officially a minesweeper, but it was actually an all-purpose vessel. When we were not sweeping mines, we were on patrol duty for submarines and performing escort work for large ships.

One time, we were sweeping a harbor to destroy defensive mines so that they could be replaced with new ones. It was a summer day, and as the cable was being reeled in to complete the day's work, one of the men standing at the fan tail of the ship swallowed hard when he saw a mine had tangled in the cable. The cable was being reeled in and, so was the mine. By the time the winch stopped, the mine was only a few feet from the side at the rear of the ship. Half of the mine was on the surface and we could see its greenish horns wrapped in seaweed. There was no assurance the mine would not explode if one of the horns struck the side of the ship. It was an ugly looking piece of devastation. Except for three of us, the captain immediately ordered all hands to abandon ship. Lifeboats were launched and we were left alone to deal with this life-threatening situation. Two of the men were to cut the cable between the mine and the side of the ship. I was to keep the fantail of the ship away from the mine. The fact the water was choppy hindered our efforts and, for some time, we watched helplessly as the mine bounced up and down, hoping it would not contact the side of the ship. I was unable to see much of what was going on insofar as the men on the life rafts. I had my hands full keeping the tail of the ship away from the mine. After what seemed an eternity, the mine was cut loose and disposed of by rifle fire. We still felt some of the force of the mine when it went off. Usually, the mines would send up a cloud spray of water into the air reaching a height of about 100 feet. The captain did a masterful job in handling the entire situation and, later, wrote the Navy Department to make an entry in our service record that was highly complimentary.

The citation read:

> "Louis J. Ruchek, Signalman Second Class, is hereby commended for his courageous performance of duty while his ship was engaged in the sweeping of a defensive minefield. With no regard for his own personal safety and risking certain destruction, he assisted in the removal of a live mine from the sweep gear of the ship."

Honestly, I don't consider it a big deal when comparing it to what some other sailors, soldiers and airmen went through. If you want to talk about bravery and danger in the service, I think of the belly turret gunners on crippled bombers when they were trapped inside the bubble and the plane had to make a belly landing. I think of the men in submarines who had to contend with depth charges exploding all around them. I think of men trapped in steel tanks, and the men who flew fighter planes. Airmen on bombers took a terrible beating in their flights over enemy territory. I have a cousin, John Pear, who was a waist gunner on a bomber. He was lucky in making the twenty-five flights over Germany after which he was sent home to be an instructor. John told me that during the long six hour flights they had to chatter the machine guns periodically to keep them from freezing up in the extreme cold. Most servicemen will agree that the most dangerous of all duty belonged to the infantry soldier who landed on the beaches of the South Pacific and in the European theatre and who faced deadly gunfire from the enemy. Every single one of these men should have received a medal. There were the Rangers who climbed ropes to the tops of cliffs with the enemy firing down on them and soldiers who spent every day in fear of a Charlie ambush in the jungles of Vietnam. Every service—from the Coast Guard to the Army had tasks involving danger. It's unfortunate that so many brave deeds went unrecognized. I can't help but think of all of this when I see someone burning the American flag and I have to tell you here and now how angry I get.

We were instructed not to discuss mine equipment aboard the ship with civilians. When we stopped at small coastal towns to refuel, a number of the local residents would come down to look at our ship. They were always puzzled by the big hammer-looking device on the bow of the ship and would ask how we used it. We couldn't tell them that a jackhammer inside of the head made noise like a ship's propeller that would set off a mine. So, some of the fellows, with tongue in cheek, would tell the local people that we used it when we found a Japanese submarine on the surface—that we hit the submarine with the hammer and beat it to death.

One spring day, when we were in the Bering Sea sweeping for mines, we happened to set several of them off. The underwater explosion was very forceful and lots of fish surfaced after the blast. On one occasion, there was a run of salmon around the ship after we set the mine off. We stopped

This mine went off a little close to the ship.
Yes—it would rock our ship.

the ship, put a boat over and hauled in hundreds of pounds of fish. We got the idea of trading the fish to the Army base at Adak. We traded the fresh salmon for cans of food that had been out in the weather. The cans were intact, but their labels were all missing. We took our fish in a dump truck and brought it to the Army after which we loaded the entire dump truck with cans of food without labels. For many months, the cook would open the cans hoping to find food that could be used for our meals. The cook would come to us—shaking a can by his ear. He would ask us to do the same, and tell him what was in the can. It wasn't unusual for the cook to be looking for a can of tomatoes and end up with sauerkraut or something else. There was considerable trading of fruit dishes among us during those meals. Dining in those days was truly an adventure in itself.

Standing watches was our main duty when we were underway. My watch was on the flying bridge with its large blinker lights that I used to signal the captain's messages or receive messages from others. At times, it was difficult to read the blinker light signals from other ships, particularly in bad weather, or if there was not a good blinker man on the other ship. The regular Navy signalmen who had been in the Navy prior to the war were well trained and absolutely tops in receiving and sending signals. A good signalman would open his blinker indicating that he could receive a message without blinking after receiving each word.

When we were tied up at docks and I was standing watch, I would call a signalman from another ship with the blinker light and shoot the breeze. It was good practice and made my watches more interesting.

Actually, I had it pretty good. A lot of my watch was in the pilothouse. My shipmates had to stand in the open weather and endure the sleet and wind. One time, I had a flying bridge watch at midnight. I was awakened from my bunk, got dressed in warm clothing and proceeded to the pilothouse. When I

I spent two years on this mine-sweeping ship.
I spent most of my time operating the blinker lights on top of the flying
bridge or on the helm. (1942)

got on deck, I lost my grip on a ladder going to the pilothouse
when a huge wave hit the ship. I was picked up by the wave
and carried over the center of the ship. I was aware I was
being swept overboard and when I reached the opposite side
of the ship, my hand caught a railing chain that was about
three feet above the deck. I hung on and was able to stay out
of danger. Had my hand not caught the chain, I would surely
have been lost at sea. It was dark and no one would have
witnessed my going over the side.

Fishing in the Bering Sea was a sport we thoroughly
enjoyed. Halibut, red snapper and salmon were plentiful,
and we always came up with good catches for our dinners.
We also caught crabs and due to all the seafood, our food
bill for the ship was always below our allowance. This
worked to our benefit because the cook would use the extra
money to order us steaks and strawberries.

This was a giant one.

We got two mines here at the same time.

There was a lot of work on the ship when we were not underway. Brass always needed polishing and the ship was always thoroughly cleaned after a big storm. There was only one occasion in the three years I was on the ship that I was able to enjoy civilian company. We were escorting a tanker and, while on high sea near Cordova, Alaska, one of our Cooper Bessemer diesel engines broke down. We had to pull into Cordova, a little fishing village with a population of about 2,000, and wait a week for parts before we could get underway. The people in Cordova were very much involved in the war effort, but they had never had an opportunity to entertain servicemen.

To show their appreciation to men in service, they really went overboard in welcoming us to their city. The bakery had fresh doughnuts for us every day and fresh milk was brought to the ship. For those who enjoyed liquor, there were free drinks at the taverns. The residents held a huge dance in our honor and the local paper reported that some of the musicians in the band would be from our ship. The paper carried a headline announcing the dance on the front page. The article urged people to come to the dance with the slogan—"They Made The Japs Dance at Attu and They Will You Too." The affair was a huge success and so much food was brought in that it was overwhelming. When we left the beautiful city of Cordova, it appeared that about half of the town was at the dock to see us off. In fact, the bartenders threw our lines off from the dock.

Actually, Cordova was the first liberty town we had stopped in for three years. Because of my length of service in the Aleutians, I yearned for a transfer back to the states for liberty and to visit my family. I spoke with the captain, who told me I could only be transferred off the ship if I was promoted to a Signalman-Quartermaster First Class.

In order to see the states again, I undertook a heavy course of hard study. Finally, I made First Class Signalman, which in the "Old Navy" took about ten years. After I was assigned my new rate, the captain called me to his wardroom and said he had some bad news for me—that I was to be transferred to another sister minesweeper across from the dock where we always tied up. This was one of the major disappointments in my life.

After about thirty-six months, I finally got back to the states where I was transferred to an aircraft carrier in Bremerton, Washington. Let me tell you, to be in the states again was like a breath of fresh air.

During the Vietnam War many returning veterans found coming home a very unpleasant experience, but not so in World War II. Let me tell you a story to demonstrate the difference.

After I was assigned to the carrier, I was given a three-day leave. I was obtaining my leave papers on a Saturday morning when a Chief Petty Officer told me that I could save a lot of time by riding with him to Olympia that morning. He suggested I hitchhike the remaining distance between Olympia and Portland. I rode with him to Olympia and he let me off on the highway to Portland. I had never hitchhiked before and, while standing near the highway with my thumb out, a Washington State Trooper pulled up alongside me and asked me where I was going. I told him that I had been away for three years, was on a short leave and on my way home to see my parents. After checking my leave papers, the trooper told me to get into his car and he would give me a ride to Chehalis, which was half the distance to Portland and at the end of his territory.

On the way to Chehalis, we mostly talked about the war and how anxious I was to be going home. When we got to the end of the trooper's territory, he said he would have to let me off. Then, he changed his mind and said that he thought there was another way I could get to Portland. We pulled behind a billboard and watched the cars go by. After a little while, there appeared a speeding car with an Oregon license plate. The trooper grinned at me and said, "I think this is your ride to Portland." We took out after the car with the siren screaming, stopped the driver, the only occupant in the car, and the trooper asked him, "Where's the fire." He asked the driver if he was going to Portland. The driver replied that he was, and the trooper said he had a friend in his car who needed a ride to Portland. The man could not get out fast enough to open the door for me to get in. We took off down the highway and he told me I had done him a real big favor. He continued by saying that the tires in the back seat of his car were stolen and he thought he was being pulled over for theft, in addition to speeding.

We talked on the way to Portland and, although he was not going to Beaverton, he took me right to my parent's doorstep. Even a crook had a hand in helping a serviceman get home. It's shameful when you contrast this with how our Vietnam veterans were treated when they came home.

Sadly, the war resulted in the loss of several young men from our small town with whom I was acquainted. A friend, Philip Balfe, went through WW II in North Africa, but was killed in the Korean War. A young Japanese man, Shinn Sato, lost his life in Europe. Another friend, Jim Wooten, was a crack sharpshooter—somewhat a Sgt. York. During the Battle of the Bulge he was sniping away at a machine gun nest from a position up in a tree. An enemy bullet caught him in the buttocks causing him to crash through the limbs of the tree onto the snow-covered ground. After the war, I teased him by saying, "You know, Jim, you mention about sniping at the enemy from a tree, catching a bullet in your rear and receiving a citation for it. I think what really happened was that you were running from the enemy and caught a bullet in your fanny." Jim would come back with a big grin and say, "Well, at least I didn't go up to the Aleutians to hide from the war and spend all the time fishing and shooting off a firecracker once-in-a-while."

Jim saw a lot of the war as an infantryman. He was first wounded at the Siegfried Line and spent three months in a hospital in Oxford, England. He said this was the best part of the war for him. When he returned to the front, he was wounded again when a German tank shell struck a concrete pillbox and sent great chunks of concrete flying everywhere. At the time he was charging toward the pillbox. He was again wounded when he was hit in the buttocks. Jim told me that when his unit was in the Bastogne area it was transferred to General Patton's command. He said the general made the remark, "By the way, leave your (expletive) trenching tools behind. We do not stop to dig in." Jim was at the Remagen Bridge at the end of the war.

Several veterans, including Jim and I, were instrumental in starting a VFW post in Beaverton and fifty years later it is still in existence.

There were other bad effects from the war. A brother-in-law, now deceased, was shot in the back as he was parachuting in the Anzio landing in Italy. The bullet lodged next to his spine and was never removed for fear he might become paralyzed. Another brother-in-law, also deceased, suffered terribly while interred in a Japanese prison camp for four years.

After spending three wonderful days at home, I went back to Bremerton to go to work on the aircraft carrier. As I recall, I had about six to eight signalmen to train. But, before I got started, the war ended. Because I had accumulated so much service overseas, I was one of the first enlisted men to be discharged from the Navy at Bremerton.

Insofar as my Navy experiences were concerned, I must say I still have a place in my heart for the Navy. It was wartime when I served, but I learned a great deal and, most importantly, I had the comradeship of the fellows who served with me. I would recommend a Navy term for any young man. You certainly learn to live and work with your peers—something that money cannot buy.

BACK TO UNION PACIFIC

I had put in several years overseas and in September of 1945, I was one of the first in a group to be discharged from the Navy. I was a civilian, newly married, anxious to get back home to Beaverton and ready to return to work on the railroad.

While I was away in the war I also gained four years of seniority on the railroad. Consequently, I could bid on a better-paying position that involved considerable over-time. I bid on a job as a material clerk on a steel gang whose main job was to keep a "blue book" that recorded the number of each rail removed and replaced in the mountain area of Gibbon and Sloan in Eastern Oregon. The "Big" steam locomotives operated on the steep grades of these mountains. It was an incredible thrill to watch those massive engines snake their way over the mountains, all the while spewing out huge steam clouds that stretched forever along the back of their mile-long trains.

There were one hundred men in the gang and working between passing trains they could lay about one and one half miles of new track in a single day.

Most of the men working on the steel relay gangs were homeless. They would work about six months, quit and then draw unemployment. This was particularly true during the cold, harsh winters.

We had a homeless timekeeper, John, who was absolutely amazing with figures. He could just look at a row of figures six across and three deep, add them and give the correct in addition in about three seconds. John was in his late fifties and prior to his railroad employment had worked an important position at an atomic plant. I was impressed with his tremendous knowledge of math and asked him why he left his job. He told me he had an independent nature and that he liked the idea of not being too responsible for solving difficult problems. He said he enjoyed the life of being homeless and being a "boozer." John was not a daily drinker, but he would work for about three months and then go on a three-day drinking binge until he actually saw snakes on the wall of his hotel room. After the three-day drunk, he was okay again for another three months, when he would go on another blast. John was a kind and intelligent man, and I enjoyed playing chess and checkers with him. He was very good at both and I played second fiddle most of the time. He had a delightful sense of humor and loved to tease. I remember when he met my attractive wife for the first time. He asked, "Why is it when a young couple gets married, one is extremely good looking and the other is just so-so?" Then he said, "Gee, you know your husband is really good looking," which, of course, made us all laugh. His jokes were always of a reverse clever nature and they came quickly.

The foreman, John and I lived in a boxcar that had been converted into living quarters with bunks, and it provided suitable living and was quite warm and comfortable at night. When it got cold we built a fire in the potbellied stove using coal for fuel. Many times during the night we would hear the howling of the wolves and coyotes that lived in the mountainous forest around us.

Cooks prepared our meals in the food car and made sure coffee and doughnuts were always available for the hard-working men. Usually, the railroad hired a married couple to cook for the men and paid them both a monthly salary. The cooks had their own boxcar, and the laborers would sleep about eight in a car. The food was always excellent and certainly one of the reasons it wasn't difficult to obtain "gandy dancers" to work on the railroad. If the food was not good the men would simply quit and drift to another railroad gang noted for having a good cook.

Our gang's cooks were excellent and I still remember the decadent raisin cinnamon rolls with homemade frosting they served at breakfast. They had anywhere from 80 to 100 men to feed and it was not easy to keep everything in order. While listening to the Republican convention I was surprised to hear that former President George Bush's father was a cook on a Union Pacific Extra Gang. Obviously, he was a busy man.

Although I was very busy keeping the records on material, I found time to work out by joining in the work with the men. Back in those days, spikes were driven through the tie plates into the wooden ties with a long handled maul that weighed about sixteen pounds. Two spikes about six inches long were placed into a hole in the tie plate and one of the men on one side of the rail would strike the spike head with the maul. The man on the other side of the rail would almost immediately bring his maul down and strike the head of the same spike. This was done with such rat-a-tat machine-gun speed that the loud noise from the separate blows sounded almost as one. The sounds were like musical rhythms. It wasn't too long before I gained sufficient speed to participate with a partner in driving spikes. The men told me I had passed the test as a gandy dancer and I could consider myself one of them. The days of the big circus gangs are gone and today the railroad uses spike driving machines that operate much faster than men ever could. When I was on the gang, we would lay about one and one-half miles of track on a good day. One and one-half miles may not seem like much, but you must remember what track we took out we had to immediately replace so the trains could continue to run on schedule.

Our foreman, Don, was tough when it came to the work. Nonetheless, the men respected and liked him. Many of Union Pacific's supervisors "came up through the ranks" and most "served in the trenches" first. Union Pacific had good supervisors and managers as well as excellent presidents during the forty years I worked for the railroad. Jeffries, Stoddard, Bailey and Kennifick certainly deserve a great deal of the credit for making Union Pacific one of the top-rated railroads in the country and, possibly the world. Also contributing to the railroad's success were the men and women who served on the board of directors—all sharp business people.

Union Pacific had a darn good safety record during the time I was employed and has continued to improve on it since I retired. When I started working for Union Pacific in 1941, I inherited an excellent railroad and when I left in 1980 it was still one of the finest. All the trainmen, engineers, maintenance-of-way workers, mechanical men and many other crafts too numerous to mention worked hard to make it so. Their loyalty and dedication to a job well done was unequaled. I feel qualified to say this because my position as a claims investigator brought me in contact with many of the employees of different departments. Today, like so many large companies that undergo mergers and acquisitions, the Union Pacific suffered a series of setbacks after its merger with the Southern Pacific Railroad. It is working its way back, however, to being the pride of the railroad industry.

While I was working with the maintenance-of-way workers, I observed gangs of Navajo Indian workers the Union Pacific brought in mostly from New Mexico. Like we have "Smith", it seemed every one of them was named "Begay." Although born in this country, most of the Indians who worked on gangs did not speak English, but spoke their own Navajo language. Union Pacific made a good choice in hiring them. They were excellent workers—nimble in their work, quick in their movements and rarely did they sustain an injury. With their sure-footedness and little fear of heights, I often thought they would have been great at working on high steel sky-scrapers. After the railroad mechanized, Navajos operated equipment such as cranes and cherry pickers. They were exceptional operators and I marveled at how well they could work their hands and feet at the same time.

Most of the Navajos would come in the timekeeping car after payday where John and I would help them mail money orders to their families in New Mexico. An interpreter told me they really appreciated the opportunity to make good money and to be able to improve the lives of their relatives in New Mexico.

The Navajos had their own rituals. Later, when I was working at Spokane as an investigator, there was an automobile accident in town and, unfortunately, a Navajo was killed. His friends and relatives chipped in and purchased a rifle, food and blankets. These items were placed in his coffin to assist him during the time he spent going from this world to the next one. His coffin was shipped back to New Mexico for burial.

When the Navajos were paid for the first time they usually bought clothing. The purchases most likely included Levi's, a black vest, a ten-gallon hat and, of course, good leather boots. A majority of the men tied their black hair up in a bun on the back of their neck. Their hair was underneath a black, tall crown, stovepipe-type hat that didn't have a wrinkle in it. They looked great.

Although they did not speak English, you could tell they were really friendly and appreciated our help in filling out various forms. Smiles go a long way in bridging language barriers.

I heard about a track worker on another railroad who, all of his life, dreamed of owning a tavern in San Francisco when he retired. He worked for the railroad for over thirty years and hardly ever missed a day of work. He toiled, sweated and skimped to save money to buy his dream tavern. He never bought lunch out, but always brought it from home. When he and his co-workers would go out, he made sure that everyone paid for their own drinks because he was fearful he might spend more on them than they would on him. Approximately six months before he was scheduled to retire, he was killed in an accident. The state received most or all of the money he had saved all those years because he did not have any living heirs. Fate can deal a cruel blow at times.

I remember what hardworking Mr. Peterkort told me when I was a youngster working in his greenhouses—"Money is really nothing. The only time it is important is when you don't have any or not enough." Also, he asked, "Does it matter if a person dies rich or poor?"

I enjoyed working on the steel gang and the pay was good. It was good for me to learn maintenance-of-way, a very essential part in the operation of the railroad. However, the over-time finally ended and I bid back to Portland where I returned to work in the Time Bureau calculating the time of the trainmen and the enginemen. Instead of paying these men by the hour, they were paid by mileage on a 100-mile basis.

One day, when seated at my desk calculating payrolls and timeslips, an elderly gentleman approached me. He introduced himself as the District Claims Agent of the Northwest Division—a job I was to hold years later. He told me there was an opening in this small department of the railroad and asked me if I wanted to work as a claims investigator. The job involved investigating accidents and settling claims. Railroad workers did not come under Workmen's Compensation and settlement for injuries was made by the railroad directly to the employee. He added that this was an excepted position and that I would be considered an officer on the railroad. I immediately told him that I was interested in trying out the job. Thirty years later, I was still trying out the job.

At the time the offer was made, I was working as a union employee and was secretary to the Chairman of the Brotherhood of Clerks. When I accepted the position as a claims investigator, I became a member of management and was no longer a union employee.

When I accepted the job as a claims investigator I really didn't know what the job required. Not only was I to work with injured employees, but the position I had to investigate any accident where the railroad was involved. Working as a claims investigator required knowledge of how the railroad operated and covered many crafts such as switchmen, engineers, trainmen, sectionmen, etc. A claims investigator had to be more or less a jack-of-all-trades. There were cases involving electrical accidents, switching boxcars, mechanical accidents, crossing accidents and injuries to passengers on trains. We also handled livestock and fire claims. Usually, we were a department that spent money in payment of claims. Occasionally, however, we would collect for the railroad— for example, a vehicle damaging our crossing signals.

When I started as an investigator, the railroad had numerous streamliners running over the system. The City of St. Louis, City of Portland, City of Los Angeles and the Portland Rose were daily trains that operated over our lines. On occasion, we would have as many as 400 passengers on one train. These trains were powered with steam engines when I first started. Then in the early 1950's the railroad went to diesel engines. This transfer of power entirely reduced fire claims because hot coals were no longer escaping from the stack of the steam engines.

The passenger trains always had something going on as far as we were concerned. Passengers would fall resulting in injury, a suitcase would drop on a passenger's head from an overhead rack or a necklace or watch would be stolen. If a passenger fell on a train and claimed an injury, the conductor wired ahead to the dispatcher who contacted a claims investigator to meet the train. The claims investigator saw to it that the passenger received medical attention, if necessary, and investigated the accident.

It was not long before I was put on call twenty-four hours a day. The railroad had to know how to get in touch with us no matter what day of the week it was, or what time of day. When we went to a movie we were required to leave our telephone number with the ticket seller and advise our railroad telephone operators where we were seated.

Claims investigators resided in cities about 200 miles apart and were responsible for investigating accidents involving employees of the railroad, as well as anything of an unusual nature involving train passengers. Before the company sold Union Pacific Stages to Greyhound many years ago, we also handled all types of claims with bus passengers. One of my first assignments was to work on cases involving Union Pacific Stages in the Mid-West. Working on bus cases involved a lot of traveling to and from accident points. Each incident had to be written up and forwarded to the main office. A complete report was required after the investigation was completed.

I investigated many odd bus accidents in the early years I worked for Union Pacific. I recall a bus accident in Iowa. One of our stages had a full load of passengers and was going uphill following a pickup. The pickup was towing a trailer with a cow in it. Half way up the hill, the trailer hitch broke and the trailer crashed into the front of the bus. The cow ended up in the lap of the bus driver.

Another morning I was called out of a deep sleep to meet a stage coming into the Omaha bus terminal. On board was a lady passenger who had fractured her arm. When I met the lady at the bus terminal, she volunteered that the Big Dipper constellation caused her fall. She seemed unconcerned about her arm injury and continued to say she fell while looking at the sky as she was going down the steps of the bus. She seemed more concerned about not locating the dipper than about her fractured arm.

On another morning, I received a call to meet the bus because there was an elderly lady passenger who was mentally confused. When I met her at the bus terminal, she looked at me, grabbed my arm and proceeded to question me as to why I was I was not at the bus terminal when she arrived. She was quite adamant that we were supposed to be married at an earlier time. She insisted that if we hurried we could still make the church service. She was treated with kindness, and I called her family requesting that they either pick her up or arrange to travel with her to her final destination.

I was handling bus cases in the Mid-West when I was called into Omaha for further railroad training. The chief in charge of our department was a large muscular man who was highly regarded throughout the country as an outstanding investigator and claims man. It was okay for him to frequently scold and criticize us, but no one from another department had better even think about it without his permission. He was extremely loyal and protective of his employees.

Of the railroad's 25,000 employees, our department had a staff of about sixty, including clerks and secretaries. Comparatively speaking, we were a very small department. The "Chief", as we called him, held a meeting to discuss various aspects of our job. I recall him saying, "When I send you out to find someone we need, I don't want you to come back without telling me where the person is or where his grave is." He also said, "If you cannot find someone, perhaps you can arrange for that person to find you."

When I was working the Omaha railroad territory, he called me into his office for a conference almost every day. He would then proceed to tell me that he was not getting enough work out of me. I was totally taken aback when he said this, as I had been working long hours—not only on the property, but also in the office. We worked six days a week and on Sundays too if there was an emergency. Being an excepted position, we were pretty well locked in on his rules.

One day, he called me into his office and, right out of the box, he made the statement that he was not getting enough work out of me. That particular morning a hobo had been hit and killed by a train. Even though I had been up half the night investigating the case, I still made it to the office at eight o'clock in the morning. When he made the remark about my work, it flashed through my mind that there was simply no satisfying this man. But before I could say anything, he said, "You know, maybe if I gave you a $200 per month raise, which I am going to do, I will get more work out of you." He then added that a promotion was in line for me in the near future. Now, $200 a month in 1951 was a huge raise. He then told me he was sending me to work out of Cheyenne, Wyoming—a big terminal—while the regular claims investigator was on vacation. It's so hard to be mad when you're feeling so thankful at the same time.

I was extremely busy working this assignment. We were transporting passengers on five trains, three of which were streamliners. Travel was heavy with the summer vacationers, when we had a problem with a passenger in Cheyenne. I met the train at that point and rode with the passenger to Sydney, Nebraska, after which I caught another train with a problem going the opposite direction. I really racked up the miles. I had railroad passes, a Pullman pass and bus passes. With the exception of one time when I went to town to the Wigwam Hotel in Cheyenne to eat a quiet breakfast, I ate all my meals on the trains.

I made many trips from the West Coast to Omaha and back again while I worked for the railroad. I attended conferences at the home office and went back to assist when there were serious derailments, etc. I loved riding the Streamliners, where I was given my own quarters, a roomette, and dined in the diner and lounge cars. These cars were exquisite and were equipped with long, high and wide windows to view the scenery. The food was extra delicious, particularly the Omaha steaks. The tables were set with real silver, starched white linens and flower centerpieces. It was very easy to engage other travelers in conversation while looking at the passing scenery of primal forests, mountains and plains at a speed

Just a few of the Railroad Passes I used
as a claims agent over the years.

of more than seventy-five miles per hour. There always
seemed to be a carefree atmosphere among the passengers
and this was particularly true in the lounge cars. All kinds of
people used the train—businessmen and vacationers, young
and old, first-timers and people who chose train travel over
any other transportation.

Later, Union Pacific added the dome car where a passenger sat in an overhead area in a bubble of glass that
enhanced and provided a complete circular view of the
scenery.

A few days before Christmas, a passenger with a guitar
led other passengers in Christmas songs in the lounge car.
Sing-a-longs were not uncommon.

Later when I was handling passenger cases out of Kansas City I would ride foreign railroads' streamliners. They
were beautiful and were effectively operated. I really don't

know how many thousands and thousands of miles I traveled by rail. I can still close my eyes and imagine being half-asleep in my roomette listening to the click and clack of the wheels as they passed over rail joints. When I boarded one of these trains the conductors usually took my roomette number just in case a problem arose with any of the passengers. One conductor called on me to assist him after a man pinched a woman on the buttocks as she walked by. She wanted to file charges and I told her we would do so by getting off the train at the next town or by wiring ahead for the police. She then suggested the matter be dropped because she didn't want her husband to know about it.

I made several trips from Kansas City to New Orleans. On one of these trips, I was the only male passenger in the rail car among twenty female schoolteachers on their way to a convention. At the end of the trip they invited me to attend their convention saying that I could pass as a senior professor. Sadly, I declined their kind invitation.

After filling in on the vacation assignment in Wyoming, I returned to Omaha to work in that territory again. When I wasn't busy handling an accident, I was in the office reading files. The chief had a program where he gave us beginners five files. We were to read the files and then write a report as to what further investigation was needed. This was sent to him or one of his subordinates for review. If we did not cover what was required the file would be returned to us for further study—and it was returned to us continually until we came up with the right answers. We called this "button hooking" files and, at times, we got pretty discouraged when the same file was returned again and again. Over time, however, I learned what I needed to know and it was rare for a file to cross my desk more than once.

The chief had a policy about not smoking in his office. I guess he was truly a man ahead of his time in that regard.

Consequently, those of us who smoked would go into the restroom or outside to have a cigarette.

One day, the chief called me into his office and asked me if I would like to have dinner with him at the Omaha Railroad Station. At that time, the railroad stations had the Harvey Girls Restaurants, which were excellent eating houses. Of course, I accepted. When it was quitting time, I went to his office and we left for the station. The chief, a physical fitness enthusiast, suggested on the way to the restaurant that we go to the Omaha Club to work out before having dinner. I said, "Sure,"—not knowing what I was getting myself into.

I had heard the chief was quite a wrestler. He was a large man and physically very powerful. Rumor had it he had wrestled with professional wrestlers. Upon arriving at the Omaha Athletic Club he fitted me into shorts, checked my fingernails and took me into the middle of the ring. I was raised on a farm and I performed a lot of hard work that left me in pretty good condition. However, if there was anything I disliked, it was wrestling. I just didn't like someone wrapping me in a headlock and choking my breath away. Even though I was young and strong, I was no match for the chief—not in the slightest. He threw me around the ring and down on the mat like a sack of wheat. After he threw me around for an hour, I didn't really care to go to the Harvey Girls Restaurant but, of course, I did.

Several weeks after the wrestling session, I stopped at the cigar counter on the first floor of the Omaha Building on my way to work and purchased a pack of cigarettes. I had just opened the pack and placed a cigarette in my mouth when I looked up and saw the chief looking straight down at me. He then said, "Oh, you smoke. I suppose you drink too?" I answered him by saying, "Occasionally," after which he said, "Well, now that I know you smoke and drink it really explains your poor performance on the mat the other night."

Fortunately, I quit smoking about twenty years ago when the Surgeon General's warning appeared on the cigarette packages.

I think he had some second thoughts about how he treated me at the cigar counter and in the ring because he called me into his office and said he had kept me on the road a lot longer then he had planned. He said I would be going back to the coast in the near future. He then instructed me to go to the Nebraskan Clothing Store and contact a suit salesman to buy a suit. The salesman picked out a beautiful light blue suit that was one of the best wearing suits I ever had. When I reached for my wallet to pay for the suit, he told me the suit was already paid for. Later, when I thanked the chief for the suit, he pointed out that he did not want anyone to know about it. After that, I had some real good conversations with him.

Although the chief was a rough and tumble individual, he was very intelligent and well liked by the railroad president, Mr. Jeffries. Because of this, he was able to operate the department as he saw fit without outside interference from other departments.

True to his word, the chief promoted me to Claims Investigator for Eastern Washington and Western Idaho after the summer passenger vacation rush was over. This resulted in my move to Spokane. My wife's home was in Spokane and she was quite pleased to be moving back near her family.

It was now 1950 and, although the bulk of my work involved Union Pacific Railroad cases, I also found myself handling cases involving Union Pacific Stages and the Yakima Valley Transportation Company, Yakima's city buses. I was also assisting the great law firm of Hamblen, Brooks & Gilbert in trials.

In one case, a semi-truck jack-knifed and smashed into one of our Union Pacific Stages that was traveling up Lewiston Hill on an icy day. There was a downgrade of about five miles into the City of Lewiston and extreme caution had to be used not to skid on the hill's icy sharp curves. Unfortunately, the accident resulted in deaths and serious injuries to some passengers, and the case required considerable work because it involved a long distance bus.

I also assisted in handling accidents and claims arising out of the operation of the Camas Prairie Railroad, a feeder line for Union Pacific and the Northern Pacific Railroad. During my tour of duty at Spokane, the movie "Breakheart Pass" starring Charles Bronson was filmed on the Camas Prairie Railroad. One of my friends, a trainmaster, directed the train operation in the movie, which included a caboose going over a cliff into a three-hundred-foot deep canyon. The movie crew was impressed with the trainmaster's handling of the trains and, without his knowledge, paid his union dues as an actor and then informed him he had a part in the movie—the role of the conductor who was stabbed to death by the villain. I have watched this movie several times and have seen my friend stabbed at least two or three times. After the movie I would tease the trainmaster, who was also my neighbor, that I didn't want to walk with him because I would be too busy looking over my shoulder.

The movie was shot in the foothills of the Bitter Root Mountains near Arrow, Idaho, where there is usually considerable snow. Wouldn't you know, however, at the particular time they were shooting there was very little snow in the area and artificial snow was brought in for some of the winter scenes.

On the Spokane Territory, we had many gangs working as Extra Gangs, Signal Gangs and Maintenance Crews. The men who worked on these gangs often had a wanderlust nature. One of the men on the gang was killed in town off duty and after checking, I found he had an address of a lady in a small town in Iowa. I checked with the telephone operator in that town and was able to contact his sister. I delicately told her that her brother had passed away after which she said, "Oh, I thought he died years ago."

I enjoyed working the Spokane Territory and was there for nearly five years. My work often took me into Northern Idaho and, at times, into Montana. Nearly all of my travel was by train—The Great Northern, The Northern Pacific and The Milwaukie Road. All of these trains traveled through scenic country with beautiful lakes, majestic mountains and pine tree forests. Fish were plentiful in the lakes and the region teemed with wildlife. When I lived there, the Spokane Valley in the Greenacre area was mostly fruit and wheat country. Now the entire valley of orchards and fields, like many cities, has been converted into shopping centers and housing.

People were generally friendly and helpful. This was particularly true of the down-to-earth people in Montana when I told them I was investigating an accident and would appreciate anything they could tell me anything about it.

I remember making a call in Butte, Montana. When the housewife came to the door, I introduced myself and told her I would like to discuss a railroad incident with her husband. I had received information that he was a witness to the accident. The lady said this was not possible because her husband had gotten into a fight at the football game several nights previous and was cooling his heels in jail. She said he would not be out of jail for awhile and told me the date. The amusing fact about all this is that she gave me this information as though her husband were down at the Elks Club or off somewhere playing pool. I told her I hoped her husband's team won, to which she replied that this was what the fight was all about. She then made arrangements with the police for me to interview her husband in jail.

Around this time, I got involved in "The Great Uranium Hunt." It all started with an employee of the railroad who had been involved in one of my cases. I met him some time later and he asked me if I wanted to get rich. I told him I didn't see anything wrong with that and asked him what he had in mind. He then said I was a special friend and he had secret information about the location of an unbelievably huge deposit of uranium. He said this deposit was in a forested mountain range in Montana and he was the only one who knew about it. Although he was quite secretive about this information, he pointed out that he wanted to form a three-way partnership with the third person being anyone I selected. Although I had considerable doubt about all this, I thought it would be an experience to go with him and at least I could say that at one time I went prospecting for uranium. Also, there was always that slim possibility of "hitting the jack-pot." My friend seemed to be a regular guy, normal and sin-cere, so I got in touch with one of my other friends, a rail-road-building engineer, and promised him a third share in this possible forthcoming wealth. So one Saturday, after se-curing permission to be off for the day, we loaded the stakes, Geiger counter and tools in my car. We were on our way to cut a fat hog and become enormously wealthy. After driving 250 miles from Spokane, my friend appeared to be rather unsure as to what roads we should take. Finally, when we approached a small mountain area he said to stop the car. He then pointed out a mountain and said the uranium deposit was about half way up the mountain. We wondered how on earth we would get up to that area. Well, after searching for a road that would take us up the side of the mountain, we fi-nally located an extremely rough logging road. Finally, we could drive no farther. We continued on foot, walking up-ward, carrying the tools, the stakes and the Geiger counter. We then came to a cold mountain stream about twenty feet across which, unfortunately, we could only cross by walking on a slippery log which had fallen across the stream. After nearly tumbling into the water several times, my friend and I made it across. My engineer friend was not that lucky. When he got to the middle carrying most of the stakes, he slipped from the log and fell into the shallow water.

The two of us got serious with our partner and ques-tioned if he really knew where he was going. It was only then that he owned up that he had actually never been in this area.

But he followed that confession by saying it appeared to be just like the area in his dream where he had found all the uranium. Of course, our Geiger counter revealed nothing and this was the last straw. We turned around, walked back to the car and began our long empty-handed drive home. However, when we were going down the rough logging road a rock struck the oil pan of my car and I lost all my oil. Finally, after we thought we would be stuck in the woods for the night, a nice guy in a logging truck happened by and offered to tow us to the nearest garage. Here again, people went out of their way to help us, even though they were somewhat mystified about our trip. After all, they had no knowledge of uranium being in the area. I am most certain they all thought we were a bunch of dummies because we were out there looking for uranium with the facts we had. We did not dare tell them that all this resulted from one man's dream. What we didn't know (which was very unfortunate for us at the time) was that our friend would be taken to a mental hospital about a month after our search for the uranium. I guess we should have recognized that he was not normal in his thinking when he asked the truck driver who towed us to town for his name and address so he could hire him to transport the uranium to a smelter.

Later, when I bumped into my friend, the engineer, I told him that I had another mining venture that he might be interested in. This time it was a gold mine, and all he would have to bring was a swimsuit. I'm sure I do not need to spell out his response.

There was a similar incident. He was a maintenance man in the building where my office was located. Occasionally, he would come in and chat with me for a few minutes about the weather or some event in the newspaper. He appeared perfectly normal until one day he told me he was upset with the police. A few days before, a lady had been murdered in a brushy area outside of the city, and the incident was headlined in all the local papers. The maintenance man told me that he had informed the police how they could catch the killer. He went on to explain that he had been to the area where the lady was killed and had found orange peelings there. He said all the police had to do to locate the killer was to find out where the oranges were purchased and the clerk could give them a description of the killer. I asked him if he had gone to the police to give them this theory. He had gone, but they had not been very receptive. About a month later, the maintenance man committed suicide. Until he visited my office espousing his orange peel theory, he had appeared quite normal. After his death, they discovered he had a brain tumor that most likely contributed to his odd behavior. I found myself thinking how anything can happen to anyone at anytime.

I investigated an interesting case in Northern Idaho. At that time, we had a passenger train that traveled from Spokane to Wallace, Idaho—a distance of about 100 miles. The train would depart from Spokane, arrive at Wallace, wait for five hours and return to Spokane with passengers, traveling through the wilderness and around beautiful lakes. Lake O'Gara near Springston, Idaho, was one of the lovely lakes.

A seventy-five-year-old retired coal miner lived in the mountain area several miles from Springston. He was more or less a hermit, and only came to town occasionally to pick up supplies. To travel from his cabin to Springston he walked from his cabin to the railroad track and on to town for quite a number of miles. It was a long walk and he would arrive in Springston one day, buy his supplies and return to his cabin the following morning, using the railroad tracks part way. He had one physical defect—he had lost part of his hearing when he worked in the mines. When leaving Springston and returning to his cabin one day, he started out in the morning walking between the rails of track used by our passenger train. He reached the area near Lake O'Gara and was walking away from our train that was approaching him from the rear at about thirty-five miles an hour. Unfortunately, an oil leak sprung in the cab and both the fireman and the engineer started to immediately tackle the problem. In the few seconds they were concentrating on the oil leak, the train rounded a curve and the engine struck the man knocking him in a snow pit about ten feet below the track. Unaware, the train continued on to Wallace. During the train's five-hour stop at Wallace, the old miner regained consciousness and, although he was injured, realized that in order to be seen by someone he had to crawl out of the pit and onto the track. He also knew that if he remained in the snow pit he would freeze to death that night. His chances of being seen were remote, even if he got back on the track. He struggled with all his remaining strength up the bank, made it up to the rails and passed out between them. Yes, unbelievably, it happened again. The train was making its return trip to Spokane and, after rounding the curve, they could not avoid striking him again. Immediately after the second accident, the injured miner was carried to the passenger car and taken to the medical center in Springston. He was alive and his injuries consisted mostly of broken ribs. He was featured in Ripley's "Believe It or Not", stating that the ex-miner was the only man they were aware of to be hit by the same train twice in one day and live to tell about it.

At the time of this accident, the engines on the trains consisted of steamers equipped with "cow catchers" in front and, in this particularly case, each time the elderly man was struck the catcher shoved him to one side. This accident occurred in 1950 and it wasn't until 1960 that trains became powered by diesel engines.

I was working in my office at the Spokane Union Station one day when a middle-aged man walked in. This was in 1950 and we still operated passenger trains in and out of Spokane. The man said the railroad had lost his suitcase filled with many valuable items and keepsakes. He mentioned that he had managed a huge ranch for millionaires in Texas and had accepted a similar position at a big ranch in the middle of Eastern Washington. His suitcase was defi-

I was traveling back to Spokane when I came upon this
accident scene involving a steam engine and a diesel engine.
The two trains met head on, each traveling about twenty miles per
hour at the time of impact. The Union Pacific was not involved.
The railroad involved is no longer in existence. (1952)

This is what a steam engine looks like after a
head-on collision with a diesel engine.

nitely on the train when it left Portland, but was lost somewhere between Portland and Spokane. He also pointed out that the railroad was responsible for his loss and that he should be fully reimbursed for its contents. There was something about this fellow—he had a way with words that made you want to believe him. He was a real smooth talker. I pointed out that his luggage was not checked, consequently there was a big question about any payment for the loss of the suitcase. He then threatened he would retain an attorney, after which I had him fill out a claim for his suitcase and its alleged contents. Whether he was going to retain an attorney or not was immaterial to me. I told the man that I would get in touch with him at the ranch where he was going to work. He had estimated the contents in the suitcase to be valued in the neighborhood of $3,000 pointing out there were articles he would be unable to replace.

After he left my office, I wired all the section foremen between Pendleton and Spokane to keep an eye along the tracks for the missing suitcase. As luck would have it, a suitcase kept together by ropes was found alongside the track near the right-of-way fence close to Ayer Junction. Obviously, someone had intentionally thrown the suitcase off the train. I had the suitcase shipped to Spokane and waited for the man to call. When he called several days later, I told him that I had good news for him and for him to stop in the office the next day. He was waiting at the door when I arrived at work the next morning. When I showed him the suitcase, his jaw dropped and he said it was not his. I told him that in view of the fact it was not his, we would keep it and if he brought an attorney into the picture we would bring out the contents to see if it was his. Without saying another word, he grabbed the suitcase and out the door he went.

I thought this ended the matter, but about a month later a middle-aged lady came into my office and brought up this man's name. She explained that, after meeting him for only one night, she had loaned him several hundred dollars, which he had not repaid and she was seeking information as to his whereabouts. She said he had mentioned that Union Pacific owed him a lot of money on a claim. I called the owner of the ranch with whom I was acquainted and asked if the man was still working for him. He was, and on that day he was on manure wagon detail. I don't know if the lady ever got her money back. I was certainly not surprised to find him on the manure detail instead of managing a 5,000-acre ranch.

Speaking of fraudulent claims, on one occasion I received a written claim for a prize bull that was killed by a train. In parts of Northern Idaho it was prima facie negligence on the railroad if an animal was killed on railroad right-of-way. In other words, the railroad was guilty unless proven otherwise. If a gate had been left open at a cattle crossing it was up to the railroad to prove who left the gate open. In any event, I paid the farmer a fair amount for the bull after I spoke with the engineer who had been operating the engine that killed the bull. The engineer told me that he was rounding a curve when he saw the bull lying down between the two rails. He told me the bull never moved a muscle as he approached, even though the engineer was sounding the whistle and the bell. This is not so unusual. Livestock that got on the right-of-way would often only look up at the approaching train instead of moving into the clear.

About six months went by and a man came into my office and said he had worked for the rancher I had reimbursed for the loss of his bull. He said he got into a family dispute with the rancher and that he wanted me to know that the bull I had paid for had died in the pasture. He said they moved the bull to the railroad track to be struck by the train. Later, I confronted the rancher with these facts. He also received quite a lecture. I told him I knew of instances where the hip bone of a bull got underneath the trucks of the engine and derailed the train. Had this happened in his case he would have been in very serious trouble. When I pointed out that he actually stole the money, he could not get his checkbook out fast enough to reimburse the railroad.

Jim Kenyon, a claim agent with the Camas Prairie Railroad, had a similar case because a farmhand had a wage dispute with the rancher.

About sixty miles from Spokane our railroad track ran for miles alongside a large cattle ranch running about 2,000 head of cattle. The owner of the ranch employed about ten cowboys and while I was talking to him the cook rang the dinner bell. The rancher insisted I have lunch with him. I thanked him, but told him I had a heavy schedule that day. He kept insisting until I gave in. I'm glad I did; it was the best lunch I ever had—a very fine steak (gee, I wonder where it came from) and homemade apple pie. I did a lot of adjusting with this rancher, and we finally made an agreement that instead of calling on him to pay for each animal killed, we would wait until about five or ten were involved and then we would discuss the claim. The rancher would always tease that the animal we killed was the best and biggest in the herd. I would counter that with 2,000 head of cattle, he certainly knew his cows.

Once, I was discussing a case with John Erlichman, a Seattle attorney who was close to President Nixon. I told him that he had set a pretty high value on his case. He countered this with a grin saying, "Don't you fellows on the railroad always pay for the heaviest or best cow in the herd."

The ranchers were our neighbors on the right-of-way and it was important that the railroad treated them fairly. We attempted to handle these cases promptly and to each party's mutual satisfaction.

Speaking of livestock claims, years later when working the Seattle territory, I went to a house just outside a small country town near Seattle to handle a claim for several cattle killed by our train. The husband drove trucks and his wife was busy raising children. At the time I contacted them, they had raised about twenty children—none of them their own. I

asked her where all the children came from and she told me
that they started by taking in several children to raise many
years before. It grew to a point where mothers and fathers
would leave their children to be raised by this wonderful
couple. She said a technical engineer for an aircraft company
appeared at their doorway one night with two young boys
about ten years old. He told them that he could not take care
of the boys properly and that he wanted a good home for
them. This lady took me down to the basement of their house
and showed me where she and the children had canned about
three hundred quarts of peaches. She said the children were
raised as a family and that everyone participated in picking
and canning the peaches. This wonderful couple had been
doing this for many years and their home was built and paid
for by the children they raised who were now adults. One
could taste the love in that house. The two beef animals that
we had killed on the right-of-way represented their main meat
supply and after visiting with this great family, I stretched
the payment for the animals as much as possible.

I investigated a case in the Spokane Territory involving
a driver of an automobile that struck a steam switch engine at
a city crossing. The driver had just been in the liquor store
and purchased a bottle of whiskey. He went to his car, drank
a considerable amount of the liquor and proceeded to the railroad tracks about a block away. Unfortunately, a steam switch
engine was traveling across the street and there was a collision. The accident resulted in injuries to the driver who later
sued the railroad for damages. Our attorney at that time was
Frem Nielsen, now a Senior Federal Judge in Spokane. One
of the main points of the trial was whether the liquor had
time to impact the man's driving ability in that short period
of time. Both sides had experts testify to the time element it
would take for the liquor to affect him.

The trial lasted about a week and was tried in the dead
of winter. It was very cold, but a man with a red nose that
looked like he got along real well with liquor came to the

trial every single day. He was always the first one in the courtroom and he always sat as close to the jury and judge as possible. Apparently, he did not want to miss anything going on in the trial. Because the case involved liquor, we thought he was also interested in the time element of the effect of liquor. I am sure that the plaintiff's attorney wondered who this man was and whether we had anything to do with this chubby red-nosed gentleman. I am sure he also would have preferred that this man sit away from the jury but, of course, no one could do anything about it. Finally, when the jury was out I met the elderly potbellied gentleman with the cherry nose and questioned him about his interest in the trial. He confessed he was homeless and that he came to the trial because the courtroom was always warm and that it was interesting to hear the cases. He tried all the courtrooms and always picked out the warmest room with the most interesting case. He said he was hard of hearing and sat as close to the jury as possible. The fellow was quite amusing and talkative so I asked him what kind of verdict he thought the jury would bring in. He answered promptly, "The jury isn't going to give a damn cent to the plaintiff." As it turned out, he was correct.

A number of months later, Frem was trying another case in another area and who sat close to the jury again? That's right—our little red-nosed friend. At the end of the trial when the jury was out, he again correctly predicted the outcome of the trial. His only complaint about the trials was that one courtroom was a lot colder than another. Interestingly enough, he enjoyed watching Frem working and made it a point to be at his trials. After all, who wouldn't? Later, I teased Frem as to where he was hiding his cheerleader when he was not working a trial. Frem was a super attorney and a real delight to work for.

One of our passenger trains struck a semi-trailer on a crossing. The trailer was loaded with all kinds of sporting and office goods such as skis, winter clothes, guns, typewriters, etc. The steam engine crashed into the trailer and the trailer was shoved down the track for about a block with articles flying from the trailer and landing on the right-of-way. A highway ran parallel to the railroad track and shortly after the accident happened, a driver of a car stopped on the highway and ran to the right-of-way. He loaded his arms with articles that had flown out of the trailer and placed them in his car. He started a chain reaction because many cars stopped, and the occupants carried articles from that accident away.

The night after the accident, federal officers (this was an Interstate Commerce case) announced on the small town's local radio station that the people who had taken articles from this wreck would be prosecuted under federal law. The officers handled the situation wisely by adding that if the articles were returned to the scene of the accident between ten o'clock and midnight that night, there would be no charges filed against any person who returned his ill-gotten goods. That night, I went to the scene and watched car after car stop with the drivers returning articles they had taken from the right-of-way. A lady with a baby in her arms returned a pair of skis. It turned out to be a very effective announcement.

I investigated a case where a lady was driving and her automobile struck our train at a crossing in a small city. I went to interview her to obtain her statement in the trailer house where she lived with her two minor children. In her statement she mentioned that the crew had been drinking and this caused the accident. I spoke to the police who advised me that *she* was the one with liquor on her breath, and not a member of the train crew. After finishing my business with her, I went to work on other cases in the area. At about eleven o'clock that night, I was working on reports in my hotel room when I decided to go to the restaurant to have a cup of coffee before going to bed. I took a booth in the restaurant and was drinking coffee contemplating what I was going to do the next day when the lady I had interviewed that day walked into the restaurant. What a transformation! When I was with her in the trailer earlier that same day she looked quite average. But now, at the restaurant, she was stylishly dressed and was a real knockout. She did not notice me and took a seat next to two businessmen at the counter right across from my booth. The two men were talking and paid absolutely no attention to her. Suddenly, in walked a man about 6'5" and weighing around 250 lbs. He wore a cowboy hat and cowboy boots. From the expression on his face you could tell he was mad. He looked around and spotted the lady, went over and yelled in her face, "Why are you not home watching the kids? I ought to beat the hell out of you and these guys you are with." The two businessmen did a double take and their mouths flopped open in complete surprise. After having said what he came to say, the large man spun around on his heels and proceeded to leave the restaurant. Leave it to some high school kids in the booth behind me to stir the pot. One of them yelled, "Oh, yeah." The big cowboy promptly turned around and started for the two businessmen. They did not wait to explain that they didn't know the lady, but ran through the kitchen out into the street.

I investigated a bad accident at a crossing near the Oregon-Washington border. Our attorneys wanted us to video the crossing at about one o'clock in the morning—the same time the accident occurred. We arranged to use a switch engine from the Hinkle yard with the same number of cars as the one involved in the accident and boxcars on the side tracks. I waited for the train and when it finally arrived, I was completely surprised to see a petite young woman climb down off the engine. She was the first woman engineer I had ever seen on the Union Pacific Railroad. She did a terrific job of handling the engine during the taping and we would have used her at trial had the case not closed. I was glad to see the railroad open up many positions to females that had historically only been handled by men.

There is a small town in Idaho that was the end of our branch line from Spokane. Our lead employee in this town was a man by the name of Alex, and he pretty much represented the railroad in the community. When I came to town I always went to Alex's house and talked to him about the cases I had to work in the area. He knew almost everyone and it was a delight for him to help me find people, witness signatures, etc.

One night I came to town and, as usual, stopped at Alex's house where his wife served me some coffee. Alex asked me what I had to investigate on this particular trip. I named a few cases and I mentioned a lady's first and last name. Alex's wife smiled and explained that the "lady" was a madam of one of the several houses of prostitution in town. The "lady" had been in an automobile that was struck by a switch engine at a crossing. She sustained a broken ankle and the report from the engine foreman indicated the gentleman who was with her was probably injured too. Alex kidded that if it were absolutely essential that I contact her, he would be happy to accompany me for support. His wife laughingly told him that if he ended up going with me to visit the *madam* that he would have to use his own money—he wasn't welcome to the money in their cookie jar.

I told him I would discuss this situation with my boss in the morning since I did not relish the possibility of my being seen going into a house of prostitution, particularly if it got around the railroad. On the other hand, we did have a rule that every case had to be investigated if a serious injury was involved. My boss washed his hands of the matter by saying the decision was mine to make.

I called the lady and politely requested she meet me at a nearby restaurant. She said she could not go down the stairs on crutches and suggested I just come up to the rooms.

Taking the bull by the horns, I decided I wasn't going to fool around about seeing her so with my typewriter and briefcase in hand, I climbed the stairs to the doorway and rang the bell. An attractive girl answered the door and ushered me into a small room where a jukebox was playing a Bing Crosby tune, "White Christmas." I had only been in the room for a few minutes when the very attractive madam walked in on crutches. I obtained her statement in which she said she was a passenger in the car. When she and the driver heard the engine whistle the driver panicked and slammed on the brakes. She was thrown forward and, because her legs were crossed, her ankle snapped. She stressed the injury occurred prior to the impact and added that the train crew did everything correct in blowing the whistle, ringing the bell and moving at a safe speed. She gave an honest report and signed the typewritten statement. Later, I contacted the driver of the car. He also gave an honest report, stating that the engineer had really been leaning on the whistle and the ringing the bell prior to impact. I could only imagine what could have been so distracting that the driver did not hear all the commotion of the approaching train.

About a year later, I was returning from this same town on the passenger train to Spokane. It was the day before Christmas and the railroad car in which I was riding carried about twenty of the "working girls" from the town going home for the holidays. We were the only passengers, and one of them asked me what I did for a living. I was happy to pass the time and told them about my family and where I was born and raised. I remember one of the girls (the prettiest) telling me that she was traveling to Wisconsin to visit her parents who owned a dairy. They were excited about seeing their relatives over the holidays. These ladies were very proper, but didn't hide their profession. When we reached Spokane (about an hour and a half later) I departed the train and wished them all a Merry Christmas. There aren't too many professions that allow you to spend several hours being the only male making small talk in a railroad car among a group of "Ladies of the Night."

Years later, I read in a Portland paper that the last red light house in the town was closed and that an era had come to an end. The article also pointed out that the lady I had contacted had purchased the uniforms for the high school band for many years.

The only other experience that involved prostitution happened later when I was working out of Kansas City. Claimants were often scattered throughout the south and other states.

We received a letter from a man in Kentucky who advised us he had injured his back working for the railroad. He resided in one of the larger cities in the state—at least his address on the envelope revealed this information. I attempted to call him but was unable to contact him by telephone because he had an unlisted number. On one of my swings through the state from where the letter originated, I went to the city to contact this individual. I took a taxi from the train station to the address on the letter and found myself in front of a large colonial brick house on a wooded corner lot. I rang the doorbell and a lady in a white uniform asked me in. She apologized, stating that she was busy but that she would be with me in a minute. She led me to a large living area and left the room where four or five young fellows who looked like college students were playing cards. As I sat in the soft chair waiting, quite frequently the young men would look at me and smile. Finally, I spoke up and said, "It looks like you fellows are having a good time playing cards and drinking beer." One of them then answered that, although they were having a good time, I would have, "A helluva lot better time," after which the group heartily laughed. About that time, the lady in the white uniform returned. Because the man had complained of a back injury, I naively thought the lady in white was a chiropractor. I stood up and extended my hand to shake hands. I began by saying, "I am Louis Ruchek and I work for Union Pacific." Before I could say anything about the man who wrote the letter, she interrupted me by saying, "That's nice. We get railroad men in here occasionally, but I don't ever remember one from Union Pacific. Now, do you want a blonde, a brunette, a redhead…or do you want to see all of the girls?" Needless to say, I was taken quite by surprise. I explained the real purpose for my visit after which she said the gentleman I wanted to see was a drifter and had left town. She smiled and said she had it from pretty good sources that there didn't seem to be anything too seriously wrong with his back. I recommended the papers in the case be filed away until such time, if ever, we heard from this man. We never did.

I covered a great deal of this territory by automobile. Driving around handling the investigations of accidents and settling claims was wonderful when the weather was good, but in the wintertime when there was ice and snow on the highways, particularly in the hilly areas of my territory, it was frightening. One winter night I had just finished working in Wallace, Idaho, and in order to get back to my home base in Spokane I had to take the highway through the Fourth of July Pass. This highway led through a small mountain range and on this particular night, I was proceeding up a hill on solid ice. I was driving slowly, but without warning the front end of my Plymouth went off the road and skidded over the shoulder down an embankment. When the car finally stopped, the wheels were pointing at the sky and I was alone in an isolated mountain area. My car had rolled about seventy-five feet and rested on a ledge. Had I been going faster, I would have cleared this ledge and would have rolled another two hundred feet. I somehow managed to get back to the highway and, after some time, flagged a passing car. So many cars went over the ledge at this particular spot, the towing company charged by the foot after $50. In other words, to get my car up to the road I had to pay $125.

Although I was kept very busy working long hours six days a week, I was not the only one. All the officials, including the superintendent, assistant superintendent and trainmasters also worked long hours to make the railroad function. There are people who believe that railroad jobs are soft touches, mainly because of the publicity surrounding the use of a fireman in the cab of an engine. These people are not giving any thought to what happens if a bad derailment or bad weather occurs. I have seen sectionmen and other employees work around the clock to get the railroad running again.

Not only do derailments require tremendous work, but floods, snow conditions, and other problems create a lot of work that has to be handled as soon as possible to get the railroad operating again. I remember when a particularly bad snowstorm stopped a passenger streamliner in the middle of Nebraska with about 350 passengers aboard. They were all fed and cared for until the train could travel again.

I can't say enough good things about the men I worked with, particularly the operating officials. They were conscientious men who devoted almost all of their time to the railroad. I recall meeting Harold Donaldson, a trainmaster, at a motel early one morning at The Dalles in Oregon when I was checking in for the night. He had been testing train crews for safety reasons all night and said he was going to get some sleep. A few hours later I was at the yard office and there he was, working on a problem that had come up an hour or two after he went to sleep. It's simply not true that railroad workers "have it easy." I've worked with the gandy dancers on work crews to the top brass of the railroad, and I know.

A great deal of additional responsibility went with the manager's position. I was active in all the lawsuits in the territory, including all the serious injury cases. One fatal accident involved a young rail worker. About six months after the accident a charming, nice young lady called on the investigator in Spokane. She identified the deceased rail worker as her little boy's father. The excellent investigator in Spokane, Ray McDeid, and I were assigned to the case to determine the validity of her claim. If the railworker was the boy's father, the boy had a large claim. While working the case, we determined that the young lady had been going with a gentleman from another state. She pointed out that it was possible that he was the child's father. We checked with the doctor in the other state and were told the baby was conceived during a certain week of a certain month. The problem was that the young lady told us she had sexual relations with one man at the beginning of that specific week and sexual relations with the other man at the end of that specific week. A doctor stated that the time of conception was very close and either man could be the father.

I contacted the man in the other state and told him that there was a possibility that he was the father of a small boy. I pointed out that it was his opportunity to find out for sure and we would pay the cost of the paternity test. The young man agreed to this proposal and blood samples were taken from the three of them — the young man, the boy and the mother. The blood samples were rushed to UCLA by airfreight. A few days later I received a notice that, unfortunately, the test had gone awry and another one had to be run. We secured additional samples and had the test redone. It turned out that the young man from out-of-state was the father. He also ended up marrying the young woman. I believe this particular case was written up in a law journal.

Even though we all worked hard there were times when we had a little fun. A great deal of camaraderie existed between us and we went extra lengths to help each other get the work done. In Spokane, every Monday, a group of us had breakfast together, discussed how the railroad was operating and how we could improve it, particularly in the area of safety. There was Joe Searles, the Bridge and Building Supervisor, a very sharp Signalman Supervisor by the name of Harold Petty, Joe Boles, a Railroad Detective, and others. One morning, Harold Petty commented that he was irritated with one of his employees who supervised a signal gang in the boondocks in Eastern Washington. He said he could not remedy the problem without causing problems, but that he was sick and tired of being the foreman's personal mailman.

You see, Harold would bring the men their mail as he was making the rounds to his work gangs. He said the foreman had written a number of letters to ten lovelorn magazines and inserted an ad stating that he worked for a good railroad, was single and was looking for a female pen pal. He intimated that the relationship could become more than just pen pals. Harold said this resulted in sacks of mail from all over the world, including women as far away as Australia.

After he left the breakfast table, the rest of us decided we should put Harold into a better frame of mind about his mail delivery problem. We asked one of the secretaries to hand write a letter to Harold stating that his signal foreman mentioned in a letter that Harold was a nice fellow to work for, and she wondered if he would be interested in being her pen pal. We enhanced the letter by including she was 5'4" tall, weighed about 110 pounds, had a 38-inch chest and had been a contestant in a beauty contest. Harold liked horses so we had her add that she was fond of horses. The letter was signed with a fictitious lady's name, and after sprinkling the letter with a lot of perfume, Joe, the railroad detective, took the letter to Lewiston, Idaho, and mailed it from there. At breakfast a few days later, Harold mentioned he had received a letter from Lewiston, all the time watching the expressions on our faces. We kept a straight face and told him to tell us about it. When Joe Boles said the letter had probably been written by a citizen because a crossing signal was not working properly, Harold pulled in his horns and changed the subject. He was obviously suspicious, but he did not want to reveal the contents of the letter and wasn't about to be kidded about it. He was no dummy and it was obvious he was proceeding cautiously. That ended the subject for a while.

About two months later, I was riding with Harold to work in a small town when he mentioned receiving a letter from Lewiston. I asked Harold if the letter was from a railroad worker or from some citizen that had a complaint about the railroad. He mumbled something and again dropped the subject. He had a strong suspicion that one of us wrote that letter and he just did not want to be set up. We later learned from a telegrapher that Harold had checked line-ups to find out where certain officials were on a certain day—the day the letter was mailed in Lewiston. Fortunately, Joe Boles did not tie-up that day in Lewiston. Consequently, the tie-up list showed that none of us was in Lewiston.

After our business breakfast meetings we asked Harold if his signal foreman was still receiving mail from the ladies. He would frown and change the subject.

About four months later, just before the holidays, we were having a Christmas lunch when Harold suddenly blurted out with, "All right you guys. Which one of you wrote that damn letter about the lady in Lewiston?" This caught all of us completely off guard. It was so unexpected we had to laugh and the cat was out of the bag. We worked hard, but those fun times cemented our friendships that much more.

Harold Petty was one of my favorite people on the railroad, as well as in private life. He came to our home for Sunday dinner on many occasions. He was a farm boy with a high school education and went to work for Union Pacific digging ditches for signal wires. He worked himself to the top as a signal supervisor of the entire Northwest Territory, and was in charge of all the signal equipment in three states. I believe he would have made chief signal supervisor on the Union Pacific if he had not died of cancer.

He had wonderful rapport with the men not only because of his superior knowledge of the intricate signal system, but also because of the way he treated the men who worked for him. He once told me that each of his signalmen was as important as the president of the railroad. On one occasion Harold was at a signal pole on the ground when one of his signalmen was at the top of the pole. The signalman had some sort of a stroke. He became tangled among the wires and was in a desperate situation. Harold immediately strapped iron hooks on his legs and went up the pole in a hurry. He cut the wires and brought the man safely down to the ground. In the process he lost a costly ring. I told him to enter a claim for the ring and I would see that he got paid for his loss, but he never did. He also did not want any publicity on what transpired on the pole.

I recall a Sunday dinner at our home. Harold was eating ice cream when our three-year-old daughter said anyone eating ice cream was a piggy. He answered her by saying that she was right; that he was a big piggy, but that she was a little piggy because she ate ice cream too. Later, they both fell asleep in a sofa chair with her cuddled in his arms. Harold willed me a diamond tie stickpin that I still have.

My son, Ron, was a student at Oregon State University when he asked me to help him find a job during summer break. I went to Harold and he immediately said he had a position for Ron on a traveling signal gang. I was pleased to inform Ron that he had a summer job with the railroad working as a signalman on a signal gang and living in a railroad car. Ron was thrilled and commented that this sounded pretty good. When he came home after his first week of employment, I asked him how he liked the job. He replied, "All I can say is that the railroad sure has a fancy title for a ditch digger. All I did all week was dig trenches for signal wires." Ron worked the entire summer, enjoying the physical work, the traveling and the money he earned to help pay for college.

Apparently, Ron inherited his grandfather's work ethic. During college he not only worked as a signalman during one summer break, but as a heavy-duty truck driver and a logger in Alaska in succeeding summer breaks. He graduated from college and now works in the circuit board industry.

When I first went to Spokane there were a number of employee lawsuits against the railroad. The company, of course, took the position that it was much better for the workman and the railroad to settle cases without lawsuits. Being a claims investigator was a difficult job because you had to walk a tightrope. If you were too much for the company the men would dislike this. If you went overboard for the injured workman the company would take notice. I believe I earned the mutual respect of employees and company representatives alike because my philosophy was to be fair as possible to everyone involved.

I loved bantering with attorneys on settlement figures. I recall discussing a settlement with Max Etter, a Spokane attorney and former college football star. When he made a demand on a case, I told him his demand had a lot of *fat* in it. In turn, he said, "Lou, I have already reduced our demand to *skin and bones*."

When I first inherited the Spokane Territory I made it a point to become acquainted with the union officials who were handpicked for the job by the men. One who represented trainmen was named George. When I first came to Spokane I made it a point to introduce myself and let him know I would appreciate talking with him if a problem arose—we could work out problems without a lot of trouble. He agreed, and during the years I worked the Spokane Territory he became a good friend even though we were adversaries.

One day I met George coming in from the end of a run. He asked me what business I had in the area and I told him that our section crew had burned weeds on the right-of-way; that the fire got away from them temporarily, but not before burning about three prune trees in a prune orchard. George asked me if I knew anything about prune ranching. I told him that I was born on an orchard ranch, but we didn't have any prune trees other than a few for home use. George volunteered that he had been born and raised on a prune farm in the area and that he knew all about prune trees. He suggested that he accompany me to assist me in disposing of the fire claim.

We drove to the prune ranch and met with the owner. As I recall, the farmer's demand for the three prune trees was in excess of $10,000. George spoke up and pointed out that he had a lot of knowledge about prune trees and then went into the cost of the upkeep of the trees, their age, the production factor, as well as the variance of the price of prunes from year to year. The farmer dropped his demand to $5,000, which was followed by more facts from George. The farmer then reduced his demand to $2,500 and, after additional talk by George, he said he would take $1,500 for the trees. George started in again to continue to bring the farmer's demand down, but I interceded and told the farmer we would pay the $1,500—a fair amount for the damage.

Later, on the way back to the city, I told George that if I had not stopped him he would have had the farmer *pay us* for burning *his* prune trees. Strangely, George said he would have continued on because he wanted to see if I would stop him, or let him go on and take advantage of the farmer. He agreed the amount paid was fair for both parties.

Somehow this cemented our friendship. Prior to leaving the Spokane Territory, George was killed in an accident on the highway and the railroad, the workmen and I lost a good friend. He assisted me by encouraging an injured worker to talk to me to see if a settlement could be worked out. He did not participate in settlement talks. He encouraged the men to see an attorney, but also talk to me beforehand. He pointed out that all should be given an equal opportunity to discuss a case.

While working as a claims investigator on the Spokane Territory and as busy as I was, I decided to go to night school at the University of Gonzaga to study law. One of my professors was a well-known plaintiff's attorney. He was aware that my work took me out of town quite frequently, but he was kind enough to give me the missed assignments and assisted me on many occasions.

Later, the railroad was involved in a crossing accident that resulted in a lawsuit against the railroad. My law instructor was the plaintiff's attorney and I was the investigator who investigated the accident. After our attorneys won the case, the law professor kiddingly told me that he wanted me to work for him—in that way I would be out of his hair.

One morning an extra gang worker (track worker) walked into my office and said he wanted to close his injury claim; he had made a complete recovery. (Railroad workers do not come under any compensation injury act such as state compensation. Because they are Interstate Commerce workers, their injury claims are handled by settling with the worker and the railroad unless the worker retains an attorney and then it is between the attorney and the railroad.) Settlement was agreed upon a certain amount—in the neighborhood of $1,500. I wrote a check out for payment, and the extra gang worker wanted to cash my check right away. He also mentioned he had difficulty in cashing checks in the past and, therefore, he wanted me accompany him to the bank about a block from the office and make sure the check was sound. He asked the teller to give him the money in $100 bills.

After receiving the money, he expressed his appreciation for the manner in which his claim had been handled. When he started to hand me a $100 bill, I told him to not even to think about it, that I was well paid by the company, and what he suggested was the last thing I would want to accept. He then invited me to lunch. I in turn told him that I was taking him to lunch, and we went to a nearby restaurant. During lunch I asked him where he was born and raised. He told me was born in Boston and that he had not been back in the past twenty years. He commented that he should go back and see his mother while she was still alive. I suggested that now he had some money it would be a good time to see his mother; that there would be no question she would be extremely happy to see him. I also told him that if he decided to go, I would obtain a pass for him on our line to Omaha and he could purchase a railroad ticket from there to Boston. He thought it was a great idea and I told him to come to my office in a day or two and I would have the pass for him.

Two days later he came in the office—I thought for the pass, but he sat down and, a dejected look on his face, announced that all of his money was gone. I wondered how he could dispose of $1,500 so fast. He sheepishly said he had gone to a tavern where he became quite intoxicated. He bought drinks for everyone for hours, and also met a lady who was very friendly with him until his money ran out. He said he was broke and wanted a loan of $5 to get back to the gang to work. I loaned him money that he repaid in a letter after his first payday. In the letter he mentioned that he would probably ask me for a pass later, but he never did.

Did I handle tragic settlements? Yes, there was an accident involving the death of a married man, and the father of three small girls. The wife was appointed administrator of the estate and was to receive the money for his death. A substantial settlement amount was agreed upon. Prior to the closing of the case, however, the mother of the wife of the deceased came to my office and said her daughter was irresponsible. She asked if arrangements could be made to place the settlement amount in some sort of a trust fund for the children. I checked with the railroad's attorneys and was told that the wife, in her role as administrator, was entitled to receive and distribute the money in any way she saw fit. Furthermore, when they approached her about the matter, she refused to discuss it and insisted she receive the money.

About a year later in a city in the Mid-West, a city detective came into my office and inquired about the amount of the settlement. When I told him the amount, he whistled and said, "Wow." He then went on to explain he was on her case for writing bad checks. I asked the detective why in the world she would do this with all the money she had been paid. He told me that she went through the entire amount buying expensive cars and other things for her friends. When she was out in taverns and bars at night, she would give out $100 bills to strangers and employees.

I intensely disliked how it ended for the children, but there wasn't anything I could do about it. I firmly believe in the use of structured settlements that pay out the amount month-by-month as an alternative. Portland attorney John Ryan and I made the first structured settlement in the State of Oregon. As stated, injury settlements were made directly by the company with the employee. There were times this resulted in rumors that the company took advantage of the employee by not paying them a satisfactory amount for their injury. I cannot verify that every claims investigator did not try to buy a settlement on a cheaper basis, but this was truly not the policy of the company. On many, many occasions the company instructed us to be fair with the employee. The railroad certainly wanted to eliminate lawsuits and recognized the importance of having the good will of the employee. The problem was defining what is "fair." There was no pinpoint rule that spelled out what each injury is worth. What would be fair to one individual's thinking was not fair to another. The settlements on the railroad generally far exceeded payments made in state compensation cases.

I recall one case where I was accused of taking advantage of an employee. I happened to know this metal worker from the shops. He sustained a minor injury and when he recovered, he came into my office to dispose of his claim. I do not recall what I paid him, but it was in the neighborhood of $1,000. He was satisfied with this amount and was given a check. About three or four hours later, I received a call from his wife. Boy, was she mad. She told me she was outraged over the cheap settlement I had made with her husband, and how I had taken advantage of him. She continued to explode saying $300 was a very cheap settlement and that he should have received at least three times that amount.

Now, I had a choice to blow the metal worker's cover and tell her what I had actually paid him, which I knew would get him into a lot of hot water, or keep quiet. The way his wife was yelling at me, she would have probably killed him. I held the receiver about two feet away from my ear and let her rant and rave without disclosing the amount he had been paid. Believe me, I was not happy about the situation and later I met the metal worker at the shop. I told him that I wanted to thank him for getting me into trouble with his wife. He came back with, "Ah, Lou, she will forget it. She doesn't know you and, besides that, I got a new fishing pole, a shotgun and a few extra dollars for spending money."

I guess he actually felt uncomfortable about the situation because he later gave me a beautiful handmade steam engine made out of copper. He brought the engine over to my office when I was out of town and left a note reading, "You know what this is for." It plays the song "Working on The Railroad" and I still have it.

Claims investigators on different railroads always kept in touch with each other. It was quite common to share stories of our odd or humorous cases.

One of the investigators from another railroad told me they had an employee who wore rank and dirty clothes to work. He said this employee's job duties involved contacting employees of shipping companies and his manner of dress bothered their superintendent. Finally, the superintendent collared the man and told him he was not criticizing him, said that he had a very responsible job, and pointed out that having such a responsible position would entitle him to dress better. Following this conversation, the employee reported to work the next day in the same dirty jacket, shirt and pants. The only change he made was that he had put on a gravy-spotted tie. Several days later, the employee came up to the superintendent and seriously thanked him for telling him why he should dress better. Since wearing the tie he felt much better and thought people were noticing him a little more. I told the railroad investigator that the man should at least get a plus for being consistent.

In this kind of business you meet all kinds of people. I went to the home of a witness to take a statement and found myself being ushered into the living room where I sat on the sofa with my feet on a dirt floor. I was most uncomfortable that there was no floor, but it certainly didn't bother the witness. He was busy taking time to show me a combination television and record player that he had recently purchased for $500 and mentioning over and over again how much his family was enjoying it. It's at times like that that you realize it's true—different strokes for different folks.

I investigated a case in Richland, Washington, for three defendants—the railroad, the City of Richland and Atlantic Richfield, the giant oil company. After viewing the crossing involved in the accident, it was my opinion that aerial photographs should be taken at different heights above the crossing to show the angle of the street over the crossing, etc. I went to the airport and hired a pilot to take me up in his plane so I could take the photographs. Once I explained what I intended to do he said he would make it easier for me to get good photographs. He then proceeded, much to my surprise, to take the door off on my side of the plane. He told me I didn't have anything to worry about because the seat belt would hold me in my seat. That didn't sound all that good, but it seemed somewhat logical so I went along with his suggestion. The wind was rushing into the cabin so strongly by the time we climbed to 1,000 feet that I could hardly hold onto my camera. We made several passes and then he tipped the plane on my side so much that my camera was pointed straight down at the crossing. Although there was no question I was getting great crossing photographs, I'm here to tell you that I was just barely hanging inside that plane in an upside down position with only the seat belt keeping me there. With my seat belt appearing to get smaller and smaller every time I looked at it, I didn't take as many photographs as I ordinarily would. I was still thinking of that thin seat belt holding me in the plane without a door as Frem Nielsen, the railroad's excellent trial attorney, was telling me the photographs were *satisfactory*. My, what I had to go through to get a passing grade!

Because my office handled all types of accidents, I received reports of all on-duty, as well as off-duty accidents involving injuries. At times, the off-duty accidents were rather odd and sometimes humorous—providing the injury was not too serious. The accident report form requested by the company had to contain an explanation how the accident occurred and it could have been prevented.

One employee was involved in an off-duty accident while riding a bicycle. His explanation as to how the accident could have been prevented was, "Driver of car should have stopped. Also, I should not have listened to my wife when I wanted to sell the bicycle the day before the accident and she didn't."

Another employee reported a chipped bone in a toe. His explanation of the accident was, "I was watching the Blazer game when Walton got fouled. I got mad and after he sank the free throw I went to kick the couch. Instead, I hit the coffee table." How the accident could have been prevented read, "Should not have kicked anything. Also, if Walton had not made the free throw, the accident would not have occurred."

We had a portly employee who assisted passengers in the train station lobby before train time. Seeing a lady in line with a lot of luggage, he went over and picked up one of the suitcases to assist her. Unfortunately, he didn't tell her first. He just assumed she needed help. While he was in a bent over position picking up the suitcase, her dog (possibly thinking the employee was taking one of her suitcases) bit him in the buttocks. He reported the cause of the accident to be, "Not calling the lady's attention to the fact I was picking up the suitcase. Also, apparently, the dog did not like the looks of my rear end."

While working at Spokane, I received a letter from a resident who lived along the right-of-way requesting payment of a $150 veterinary bill for amputation of a dog's leg. Our tracks ran next to the backyard of a home in a small town in Eastern Washington. In the morning and late afternoon our motor car loaded with men passed by this particular house, and each time a bulldog came out of the yard and ran and barked alongside the motor car.

One particular morning, the bulldog was running alongside the motor car when its front leg reached over the rail in front of a wheel of the motor car. As a result, the dog's front leg was severed. The bulldog's owner presented a claim to the railroad and I called on him one night when I was in the area. He was a family man with a wife and children. When he started to talk about the accident, the bulldog came into the living room on three good legs and gave me a mean look—as if he knew I was with the railroad. The man told me that the dog had always been a part of the family; that the dog ate with the family, slept with the kids and they just didn't have the heart to put him to sleep after the accident. He felt the motor car should have stopped before the accident, and the railroad should pay the veterinary bill, along with an additional amount for all the discomfort the family had experienced. He didn't mention the discomfort of the dog.

I told him that I was personally sorry that the accident happened, but I had to respectfully decline any payment in the case. It was obvious the dog would be considered a trespasser and that they had been warned to keep the dog off the right-of-way. After declining the case as politely as I could, the husband turned to his wife and said, "You see there? You see there? I told you right after it happened that we should have shot him." All the loyalty and love for the dog evaporated after I declined payment.

In another nearby town I settled with a lady for an injury she incurred while she was a passenger on our train.

Her husband operated a furniture store and since this was the last case I had to work that evening, I stayed and visited with him for a while. He was in good spirits and could not help but tell me his good fortune. It seemed he had been having a difficult time selling the used furniture that he took in on trades. One of the furniture dealer's friends was moving to the East Coast and had advertised the belongings from his house, including furniture, in the local paper. The furniture dealer asked his friend if he could bring some of the trade-in furniture that he could not dispose of to his house to include in the sale. His friend was happy to help out and so the night before the sale he took over many pieces. The notice "Leaving Town. Must Sell Furniture" brought a horde of people to the house the next day. The sale was a big success and the used furniture went like hotcakes at the same price the furniture owner had marked it at the store. In fact, business was so good that at the end of the day the storeowner bought some used furniture at a competitor's business. This furniture was also sold the next day. I asked the man if anyone caught on to what was going on. He laughed and said the only remark he heard was made by a neighbor who said, "I never saw so much damn furniture come out of one house in my life."

After spending five years on the Spokane Territory investigating and settling accident claims and assisting in trials, I was called to catch a streamliner to Omaha for a conference with the chief. I recall going into his office in the summertime at about seven o'clock in the morning. It was already very hot and upon entering his office I asked him what he did for heat around this place. I don't recall that he had much of a sense of humor...

I had heard that there was an opening in Grand Island, Nebraska, which was on our mainline and paid a little more than Spokane. Imagine my surprise when I was told that I was going to be transferred to Kansas City, a huge railroad terminal. I was still pretty young in 1955 and this was a big

An Investigator's Life

promotion. I would also have two assistants to help me with the work.

Kansas City was not only a big terminal from Union Pacific's standpoint, but it was also a big terminal for a number of other railroads. Kansas City was the gateway to all of the southern states for the railroads. There were about 150 trains in and out of Kansas City daily. This included passenger trains such as the Missouri Pacific Eagles, Rock Island Rockets, The Santa Fe Chiefs, the Zephyrs and the Union Pacific Streamliners.

When I went to inspect our railroad yards in Kansas City I was amazed at the size of the operation compared to Spokane. I looked at those huge switching yards at Kansas City and found myself wondering, "What is a farm boy like you doing in a place like this?" I had come a long way in a short time.

In addition to the workers' claims, there were numerous accidents and incidents involving passengers. A big portion of my work was to handle passenger claims off our railroad line. If a passenger was injured on a streamliner and the claim was too premature to dispose of, the claim would be handled by traveling to the home of the claimant or the attorney's office regardless of in what city they lived.

Over the years, I've met a number of strange characters while conducting my investigations. I contacted a man who was an acquaintance of a witness I was trying to locate. He warned me to watch myself around this particular witness—that he was "something else." He mentioned a time when he and this man were in a bar together. The witness went into the bathroom and when he came out he wanted to shake hands. He said he extended his hand but then the fellow would not let go. He finally got his hand free after which the man went into a Bruce Lee stance. He said he ignored this so the man went to the bar, got a cup of coffee, threw the contents in his face and then ran out of the bar.

I was finally able to locate the witness at a grocery store in a small town. When I told him I was looking for him in connection with an accident he saw, he said, "Oh, a private eye." He then went into a Bruce Lee stance and invited me to close in on him. I thought it was time for a graceful exit and left the store, but he followed me all the way to my car yelling, "Let's go for it! Let's go for it." When I was in my car he got halfway on the hood and continued to yell at me through the windshield. I finally got rid of him when I told him that prior to meeting him I had called the police. Something told me he wouldn't have been such a great witness anyway—he probably would have taken up his Bruce Lee stance in front of the jury yelling, "Let's go for it. Let's go for it."

One of the strangest claimants I ever had to deal with was an elderly man who walked into my office one day and informed me he had fallen on our passenger train and wanted to make a claim. He said he bumped his head on the restroom wall when our train was stopped in LaGrande. He then told me he was acquainted with a person on the railroad's board of directors. He continued on, saying he was on a Union Pacific train in Oklahoma (we do not operate in Oklahoma) when the director had severe gas pains. He treated the director by telling him to perform specific bending exercises resulting in his almost immediate recovery. He further stated that the director was so grateful that he gave him a free pass on Union Pacific. I asked him where he had received his medical training, and he replied that he hadn't attended any medical institution, but had learned to be a doctor the hard way—by practical experience.

I told him we did not operate in Oklahoma and it must have been the Santa Fe Railroad. He solved that problem by suggesting it was a Union Pacific director on a Santa Fe train. He had an answer for everything and was a quick

An Investigator's Life

thinker. This man was really serious and I was dumb-founded to later learn that he was a prominent citizen of the community.

I asked him to show me his pass but, unfortunately, he said he had lost it. He pointed out, however, that the director was going to send him another one. After listening to him for some time, I told him I would investigate his claim and that he should provide me a doctor's report on his alleged head injury. He then told me that a doctor's report would not be forthcoming; that he was treating himself.

Because every claim presented had to be investigated, I contacted the train's crew on the day of this man's alleged injury. A porter told me that he recalled this man and that there definitely was not an accident. This porter had person-ally locked the lavatory door prior to the train's arrival at LaGrande and no one was in there at that time. He also said that no injury was reported and that he remembered the man had been continuously talking to himself after the train left LaGrande.

Shortly thereafter, the man came to my office again and said, "I hate to tell you this. I have some real bad news for you and the Union Pacific. Since I last talked to you I have this ringing noise in my head which can only be cured by a doctor I know in New York." (The World's Fair was in New York.) I could not resist replying in a nice way, "Well, sir...I have further bad news for you. I have investigated your acci-dent and the facts are such that I must respectfully decline your claim." The man then said, "Oh, my goodness. Oh, my goodness. That really is bad news. That's worse than the ring-ing in my head."

Although I declined this man's claim, he would not let the matter drop. He would periodically come into my office and ask me if I had changed my mind regarding his claim. On one occasion he said, "Now, come on. Let's settle this. Tell me how close you can come to $20,000." I told him the closest I could come was *zero*. He then said, "My goodness, you are worse than Judas in the Bible. You are sending me down the Nile on a raft with no oars. Get your Bible out and read the scripture about Judas." I told him that I did not have a Bible in my office. He then banged his fist on my desk and said, "I will not deal with a man who does not have a Bible in his office." After this firm statement, he simply turned and walked out of my office.

I thought that would be the last I would see of him but, alas, he came back an hour later with a Bible under his arm. He placed the Bible on my desk and said that we could now continue talking. His first remark was that he wanted to know how close I could come to making a $10,000 settlement. By this time, I respectfully told him that there would be no payment in his case after which he said he was going to retain an attorney. He never came back and I closed the file.

It's true that I had business with a number of odd characters over the years, but ninety-five percent of the witnesses and claimants were solid people and most enjoyable.

In order to travel to the various cities in different states, I was given about ten different railroad passes along with a Pullman pass so I could sleep on trains when traveling at night between cities. I was reimbursed for the cost of the meals I had on the trains at the end of each month.

My wife and I liked Kansas City. When we were looking for a home to purchase there in 1955 there were numerous sale signs that read "For Sale—We are good neighbors." After seeing a number of these signs, I asked the real estate salesman who was with us why it was necessary to include the "We are good neighbors" phrase. He told us that this was the homeowners' way of saying that they would not sell the house to an African-American. This was news to me and I was quite alarmed that the people selling their homes were so blatant about their feelings. I also made it a point not to buy a home from someone displaying one of those signs.

We finally selected a home in Prairie Village and the neighbors were all on hand to greet us the day we moved in.

They brought friendly attitudes and orange juice, as it was a very hot August day. It didn't take us long to find out that we lived in a great party area. The neighbors always had a party going. If it was someone's birthday, it was party time. If someone bought a new car, it was party time. If an aunt or relative was visiting a neighbor, it was party time. We were constantly invited to the neighborhood parties until I made the remark that I either had to quit my job or stop going to all the parties.

A neighbor who worked for a large corporation made a direct settlement with an injured employee. He told me that their claim personnel were too charitable when settling cases involving personal injuries. Because of this practice, the claimants had longer recovery periods. Now, this was fine for him to say, but as it turned out later—it all depended on whose ox gets gored.

I was mowing my lawn one Saturday afternoon when I received a telephone call from this neighbor. He was calling from out of town to tell me that his wife had been involved in an automobile accident with a truck at an intersection. He asked if I would investigate the matter because both his wife and the driver of the truck were each alleging they had the green light. I was lucky to find witnesses who verified that his wife had the green light at the time of the accident.

About three months later, the neighbor contacted me and stated the insurance adjuster was going to visit them to close his wife's case. He then asked me what I thought his wife's case was worth. I told him I was not in the business of advising outsiders what injury cases were worth, but being a neighbor and all, I would give him my opinion. I told him there was no loss of time involved and that his wife had made a complete recovery from her whiplash injury. Therefore, I would place a settlement value in the area of $1,500. When I mentioned this figure his head jerked upward and he said, "Wow, we were thinking more in the area of $15,000."

In any event, they hired an attorney recommended to him by a friend and settlement was finally made for approximately $1,750 after the attorney's fee. I couldn't help but think "ox."

Kansas City Station was housed in a very large stone building that had quite a history. My office was on the second floor. Gangsters and G-men fought it out there with guns blazing and there are still bullets in some of the walls. The restaurant, "Harvey's," was also in the building.

There was a Santa Fe trainmaster by the name of Fred Gossett, whose office was next to mine, and sometimes when the Santa Fe Chief would arrive or depart we would go down to the station platform and watch the activity in the unloading and loading of passengers. One day, as we were watching, an elderly lady stepped down from a passenger car onto the station platform. Underneath her arm she had a small dog in a box and under the other arm she had a miniature Christmas tree about a foot high. When she was on the station platform, she placed the tree down and then placed the dog near the tree. The dog circled the tree several times and finally relieved himself on the tree. The lady then lifted the dog into the box, shook the tree, placed the dog under one arm and the tree under the other arm and got back on the passenger car. I remarked to the Santa Fe trainmaster that I thought a false miniature yellow fireplug would have worked better. He commented, "I don't know. It seemed the Christmas tree got the job done."

One day I was having lunch with a Santa Fe Claims investigator by the name of Tom. He mentioned that he had claims to work in St. Louis. I told him I also had work in St. Louis and suggested that we both take the Missouri Pacific Eagle to St. Louis on an evening, stay in St. Louis overnight and work our cases in the morning. He agreed and we had dinner on the train and stayed at the Mark Twain Hotel.

The next morning we had breakfast together and during our conversation I told Tom that one of the claimants I had to contact lived in a certain section of the city. He then spoke up and said one of the claimants he also had to contact lived in the same section. For some reason, I mentioned the lady's name and Tom spoke up and said that this was also the name of his claimant. This lady had allegedly fallen on our train going to Los Angeles, injuring her back. She also alleged she fell and injured her back on the Santa Fe Chief when returning from Los Angeles. She only reported one accident to each railroad. The medical report was addressed "To Whom It May Concern" and reported a minor back strain. Tom and I had the same report.

Was this lady a fraud and attempting to collect from two sources? I suggested to Tom that I contact her first and obtain a signed statement and he agreed.

I went to her home and rang the bell. I couldn't have been more surprised when she answered the door. I found myself in the presence of a sweet-looking little old lady. She reminded me of one of the ladies in *Arsenic and Old Lace*. I introduced myself and told her I was investigating her claim when she fell from our train. She offered me a cup of tea and proceeded to tell me about her fall on the steps of the passenger car. She said she had recovered sufficiently and would be able to settle her claim. When I asked her if she had ever injured her back before or after the fall on the Union Pacific, she answered negatively, and signed the statement. I told her I would contact her further—possibly that same day.

Tom was waiting at a nearby drugstore and, after reading the statement I had obtained from her, he left to contact her. She repeated in a signed statement that she never injured her back before or after the accident on the Santa Fe. It was obvious she was not satisfied with one false claim, but was working on two.

Later, Tom and I went to the lady's house for the showdown. I rang the doorbell and we waited for her to answer. When she came to the door and saw the two of us, she more or less went into shock. She started crying and said that she did not want to go to jail; that actually she was trying to collect twice for a faked minor injury. She begged that we forget the claim; that she had learned her lesson. I asked her if she had a history of other claims, but she would not answer. I told her that she could be charged with fraud, however, if she promised that she would not enter any false claims in the future we would put her on probation. We assured her that we now had a record, and if she presented a false claim to anyone she would be in real serious trouble. She signed a statement explaining why she was releasing both the Santa Fe and the Union Pacific from any claims.

One evening, a soldier sat across from a businessman in the dining car. Later, we learned he had been medically discharged from the service because of mental problems. The two men struck up a conversation while they were eating. Out of the blue the soldier asked the businessman if he had noticed the conductor in the dining car. The businessman said he had, after which the soldier said, "I am going to kill him with this steak knife." The businessman could tell the soldier definitely had a problem and was serious. He suggested the soldier hide from the conductor by going to his (the businessman's) bedroom on the train and locking the door. The idea appealed to the soldier so the two of them went to the man's roomette. After the soldier stepped into the compartment the other man walked out, locked the compartment and went to notify the conductor. While he was looking for the conductor the soldier realized that he had been tricked. He piled the businessman's extra suit, camera and other articles in the center of the roomette and set them afire.

Imagine the scenario: Here was the train traveling eighty miles per hour with a man locked in a compartment with smoke coming out of the crack at the bottom of the door of the compartment. Fortunately, the train came to a stop at one of the small railroad towns and a sheriff, a real Matt Dillon type with guns strapped around his waist, boarded the train. The entire affair ended with the sheriff taking the unfortunate soldier off the train for medical treatment. Later, the businessman was paid for his loss of clothing and personal items. His bravery and quick thinking most certainly helped to avoid a potentially life-threatening situation.

Another sad case was when a sheepherder boarded a train in Wyoming. He took a seat next to a window beside an elderly lady. The sheepherder talked with the lady and, according to her, appeared to be quite normal. They rode for hours in the coach car and when the streamliner was nearing Kansas City the sheepherder reached in his bag, pulled out a revolver and shot himself in the head, and slumped over on to the lady's lap. Unfortunately, when you have approximately four hundred passengers on a train, unexpected things happen. I was amazed at how stoically this nice stately woman handled such a tragic situation.

I was working late one night when the phone rang. A stranger on the phone wanted to know if we were handling the claim of John Jones (not his real name). After I told the caller that we were, he proceeded to tell me that John Jones was his neighbor. He was aware that Mr. Jones had an injury claim for a sore back when he fell in a railroad coach. He also told me that they had had a violent argument about where to park their cars. I asked the caller what proof he had that Mr. Jones' back was not injured. He replied that if I wanted proof to go out to a certain park in the city on the forthcoming Sunday. Mr. Jones was a catcher on a ball team and his team was playing for the championship. He said there was no question that Mr. Jones would play in the game.

I retained a private investigator with a movie camera. It was a perfect situation to film Mr. Jones—a movie camera at a championship game was certainly not suspicious. Sure enough, Mr. Jones was the catcher for the entire game. He also stole second base on two occasions and had several good hits. As luck would have it, the game ended in a tie and they played for another three innings until Mr. Jones' team won. He certainly didn't appear to have any kind of a bad back. Later, when I met with his attorney it was popcorn time. Jones did initially sustain a slight back injury according to the doctor and a token payment was made. However, the amount Mr. Jones received was a far cry from the amount he originally demanded.

An old time investigator told me that during the Depression a lot of fraudulent claims were presented. He proceeded to tell me that on his railroad a young female passenger claimed internal injuries as a result of a fall when she traveled on the train. The claim was questionable in that she alleged the injuries destroyed her sex life. In order to determine the true extent of her injuries, that particular railroad hired a good looking young man, gave him $200 spending money and rented a brand new roadster for him. Loaded with this equipment, the young man made it a point to meet the young lady at a dance. They became acquainted to a point where she agreed to stay with him at a lake cabin in Minnesota. While at the resort he obtained photographs of her rowing a boat and performing other physical activities. In addition, he reported her sexual activities were better than normal. Her claim fell flat on its face when the young man's deposition was taken.

In the Mid-West there was a case where a man claimed back injuries. The company he was suing hired a private investigator who mixed Chinese food with glue and applied it to the man's driveway late at night. The claimant with the "bad back" came out to get his morning paper and saw the mess in his driveway. He immediately went into his garage and returned with cleaning articles. He actually got down on his knees, also in a bent over position, to clean up the mess. While this was going on the private investigator was filming the action with a movie camera.

The man's attorney was really sharp and started to investigate the matter after he saw the movie. He traced where the Chinese food and the glue were purchased and the two businesses identified the private investigator who purchased the articles. The attorney then pleaded entrapment and I don't recall whether or not he won the case.

It's true that those who make fraudulent claims make it more difficult for individuals with legitimate complaints.

I know of a recent case where a man claimed a back injury and was receiving disability benefits. Yet, he was able to sit on a stool to play video poker games for hours on end. I contend that if he was able to do that, he should be able to perform some type of work—perhaps as a clerk in a motel where he could sit through a shift.

I knew a private investigator who was very small in stature. You would never guess he was a private investigator from his appearance. He once had a case where a man alleging a back injury lived in a house at a corner of an intersection. This investigator would drive up to the intersection in a real fancy red sports car and park on the side of the intersection. He kept a clipboard in his lap and pretended to be counting cars. People stopped and asked him if his information was being used to put in a signal light at the intersection. He told them he did not know—all he was doing was counting cars. He stayed at the intersection for several days until the man with the alleged bad back was caught on camera carrying shingles up a ladder to his roof.

This investigator told me that in the old days a great deal of his business involved catching cheating husbands and wives. The information proved very valuable in court. He would wait for the couple to get a room in a hotel. Then he would bring a ladder, place it outside of the hotel door, climb up the ladder, open the transom and quickly take a flash picture of both parties in bed. This was usually done in the early hours of the morning when the couple was asleep. He said he had an awful long wait for one couple—something like three hours. They were very active. After the picture was taken he would run down the ladder, place the ladder across the door and head for the exit. The enraged person whose photo was just taken usually came charging out of the door and trip over the ladder. This delay gave him sufficient time for an easy get away. He said this ploy worked almost all of the time.

It would appear from what I am saying that all people who are under surveillance are crooks. Not true. Investigators who conduct surveillance will often tell you that the claimant actually has a problem. This, of course, would benefit the claimant in the settlement.

I have been questioned several times whether I ever worked dangerous cases. I did. The first one that comes to my mind happened in St. Louis. An elderly lady had a claim with the railroad. Unfortunately, she died shortly after the accident, and it became necessary for me to locate her son in connection with her case. In checking around, I discovered that he was in a real tough penitentiary, and one afternoon I went there to discuss business with him.

I had to go through the assistant warden's office to have a session with a prisoner. To enter the penitentiary I passed through two huge electric gates. Each time the a gate closed behind me I thought to myself, "I hope they can open it when I am ready to leave."

After completing the business end of my visit, I asked the prisoner how he was getting along. He told me he had no complaints; that he was keeping himself clean so that he would be able to leave the prison in the near future. He also commented that the assistant warden was a regular screw (guard) that he liked, but that the warden was a damn tough screw.

Several months after my visit to the prison I was in east St. Louis to contact a claimant. He lived in a bad neighborhood and I didn't finish my business with him until quite late. I left his apartment and started up the street to catch a bus to return to my hotel.

I was a block or two away from the bus stop, on a dimly lit street. I was the only one on the sidewalk, when I noticed four mean-looking men approaching me. I did not like their looks and I knew I had a problem because they were really eyeing me.

As soon as I saw them, I removed my tie and wedding ring and stuffed them in my pocket. The men were all wearing red bandanas and long earrings. In those days it was totally strange for a man to wear earrings and could be an indication that he was a real tough individual—like the pirates of old. When they blocked my way one of them spoke up and said, "Pilgrim, where the hell do you think you are going." I knew acting timid would be a mistake so I answered that I was going to hell. One of them then spoke up and called me a nasty name and this was followed up with, "All right, where the hell did you come from?" I then told them I was at the penitentiary, naming it. One of the men asked, "What's the warden's name?" I gave his name and said that the warden was a cheap shot, but that the assistant warden, naming him, was a pretty good screw. One of the men then said, "That's right. That's what Joe said (whoever Joe was). He is all right. He is one of us." The next question was if I was going to stay in St. Louis. I told them I was leaving St. Louis in the morning before it got too hot for me and, believe me; I was not referring to the weather. They told me to take it easy. We all shook hands and they walked ahead leaving room for me to pass.

Wasn't it lucky that I had visited the prison the month before? I was unflappable when talking to the thugs, but after I had time to think about the entire episode, I was in a completely different state of mind. It wasn't hard to imagine an ugly ending.

I owed the "chief" a great deal for getting me out of this jam. He took a personal interest in me when I was hired and told me in one of our training sessions—"When you get into a tight predicament, never lose your cool and never argue because if you do, you have lost the battle."

When I first started to work in the department the chief sent me out to locate an individual for questioning. The man alleged he had worked for the Union Pacific at one time. What made this so complicated was that the employment was supposed to have occurred many years ago. I searched for this man and finally found him in a small city residing in a cheap third-rate hotel among the homeless. He was not particularly anxious in the beginning to talk to me because he wanted to speak with "the boss." I visited with him for quite some time and toward the end of our conversation he pointed out he was not too happy about being located. He pulled up his sweatshirt and showed me a row of scars across his chest, which were the result of being machine-gunned years before when he was running liquor during prohibition. It seems he offended a gang leader and one night he was taken for a ride in the country, tied up, thrown into a ditch and machine-gunned across the chest. He said that, fortunately, a friend of his followed the kidnappers' car and when they left him in the ditch for dead, his friend picked him up and took him to the nearest hospital. At the time he was brought into the hospital the doctor said he had one in 5,000 chance of making it. He was uncertain how the men who shot him felt about him being alive. He had heard through the grapevine that these men thought he should be permitted to live if he survived taking so many bullets. He didn't have any guarantees, however, and did not want his whereabouts known. After all was said and done, it turned out that he had worked for another railroad in his youth and not Union Pacific. Consequently, we were not involved.

When working out of Kansas City, I was required to cover outlying states. I rode trains to various cities such as New Orleans, Memphis and Houston to deal directly with injured claimants or their attorneys.

Another investigator and I went to Tennessee to contact a witness to a railroad accident where two railroads were involved. We found the witness living in a trailer camp. Next to his trailer sat a large dinner table with benches. While we were talking with the witness (the man of the house) our conversation came to a halt when a lady rang a dinner bell. At the sound of the bell little children popped out from everywhere and sat at the table with their bare feet on the ground. The lady of the house brought out a big bowl containing a grayish-looking gruel. This was their dinner and it didn't appear too appetizing. The children did not have spoons. They just dipped their small bowls into the large one and proceeded to down the gruel directly into their mouths. It was in the hot summertime and there were quite a number of flies buzzing around that apparently wanted their dinner too.

At the start of the dinner, the man we were questioning asked us if we would break bread with them. It may have not been the best dinner in the world, but the fact that he was kind in offering what they had was charitable. When we left, I again thanked him for his dinner invitation and for speaking with us about the accident.

A lady train passenger was eating lunch in the diner, and reported she bit into a cheese sandwich, and felt a sharp prick of pain in her tongue. The minor cut on her tongue was bleeding. Consequently, she reported the incident to the porter who in turn reported it to the conductor, who in turn reported it to me in a telegram. Unfortunately, I was out of town at the time the train arrived in Kansas City and was unable to meet with her upon her arrival at the station. She contacted me and said she had a doctor's bill that someone should pay. I told her the next time I was in her city I would contact her to discuss her claim.

Later when calling on this pleasant lady, she repeated her story. She said she was concerned because some sharp object had cut her tongue. She was also afraid she had swallowed the object. Two days later she felt a pain in her rectum and when a physician examined her he extracted a needle from that area. The needle was a regular sewing needle and how it worked through her system and stomach was a big mystery. She said the doctor thought the needle was wrapped in the bread or cheese and this gave the needle a shield as it worked its way through her throat, esophagus, stomach and intestines. When she was ready to settle her case about a month later she asked me who would make payment—the cheese company, the bread company or the railroad. I told her this was a good question, but that I had already contacted the other companies advising them what had happened so they could conduct their own investigations where the needle may have come from. I also suggested that all three of us participate in the settlement—and we did.

Along with the handling of passenger and railroad workers' claims, it was also my job to assist our attorneys during trial. This included making hotel accommodations for witnesses and arranging their transportation followed by reimbursing them for their expenses.

A particular case in Kansas City involved four defendants. This big case could not be settled before trial, not because the plaintiff and his attorneys were unreasonable, but because there was a dispute among the four defendants as to how much of the settlement each should pay. There was no other choice but to try the case and let a jury decide the issue. This trial lasted two weeks and, as expected, there was a verdict for the plaintiff. As we had assumed, the defendant who wanted to put up the least amount of money to settle the case got hit the hardest.

A case like this is a catwalk for the plaintiff's attorney. All the attorney has to do is let the defendants stand around and point their fingers at each other as to who is responsible.

I specifically remember juror number six in this case. The attorneys for the defendants had been unable to remove him by challenge because he was one of the last jurors seated. Every night after a day in court the defendants' attorneys would meet to discuss how the case was going. Not an evening went by that one of the attorneys didn't comment about the negative looks and body language that male juror number six was directing towards the defendants. The juror was somewhat disabled and walked with a limp. Wouldn't you know it, after the verdict was in we found out that juror number six was the only one who voted *in favor* of the defendants. His reasoning: "If that man thinks he was hurt, he should have been injured like me, and I didn't get anything for it."

I believe picking a jury is one of the most difficult and most important tasks an attorney has when trying a case. Attorneys for the parties are forced to make judgment calls as to who should be left on the jury and who should be taken off. They each have only three opportunities to remove jurors, after which they have no more challenges. The problem arises when an attorney removes one juror, calls another and that one is worse than the one he removed. If this was his last challenge he is stuck with the last one.

I opened my mail one morning and was surprised to find a letter from the office of the railroad's president. They had enclosed a letter from one of the railroad's important customers, a shipper who lived in one of the cornbelt states. The shipper was upset because he had found an insect in the bed of his Pullman car. He reported it as a very ugly experience and said the incident would certainly influence whether or not he would ever travel on one of our streamliners again. His letter was referred to me for handling primarily because of his importance as a big shipper with the railroad, along with the fact that we were concerned about passengers finding insects in their berths.

I called on this gentleman at his huge home. When he answered the door I introduced myself and extended my hand. He responded to my extended hand by asking me if I wanted to wash my hands. I thought this was an odd request, however, I also thought it must have been something he wanted me to do or he wouldn't have asked. He appeared quite pleased when I consented to wash my hands and that I didn't make any kind of big deal about it.

When talking to him later, I found out that he was very germ conscious and he believed that all objects had germs on them—I guess, even my hands. That is why he was so flustered about the insect in his bed.

I told the shipper that, in view of his letter, we were taking extra measures to keep insects out of our cars. I also told him how much we appreciated that he took the time and effort to notify us of his experience. He seemed quite pleased and upon my departure again asked if I wanted to wash my hands. Under the circumstances, I could not refuse. I guess you could say I left this case with clean hands. I heard later that he wrote another letter to the railroad complimenting my handling of his complaint. I'm convinced he wrote that follow-up letter because I so willingly washed my hands twice.

I remember seeing ads in magazines for schools that taught classes on how to become an investigator. Along with the ad there was a picture of a young lady getting out of a car with her skirt hiked up above her knees. On the top of the ad a sentence read, "Work as an investigator—good pay and very interesting work." Now, I have worked over thirty years as an investigator for the railroad and another twenty years as an investigator for attorneys after I retired from the railroad, and I could never see the connection between the girl with the pretty legs in the ad and being an investigator.

I can only recall one case in my entire career that would even come close to involving a sexy lady. I was trying to serve a subpoena on a lady for an attorney. I had made a number of calls at her apartment, but was never able to catch her at home. Finally, I decided to make another attempt to serve her with the subpoena early the next morning. I went to her house around seven o'clock and rang the doorbell. She answered the door in a very thin see-through negligee. I handed her the subpoena, she glanced at the paper, looked up at me, smiled and asked if I wanted to come in and have a cup of coffee. I gulped and said, "That would be nice, but I am already late in serving another subpoena." That wasn't true, but it just seemed like it was a really good time for a little white lie.

Although serving subpoenas was not a part of my work, I was sometimes called if the person to be served could not be found by the process server. Today's computers make locating individuals so much easier, but before hi-tech I had the best results when I checked the neighborhood in person. In one example, a man we'll call Mr. Mystery could not be located. I went to his last known address and talked to the nextdoor neighbor. When I asked about Mr. Mystery's activities and hobbies, they said he was an avid golfer. I then checked all the golf courses in the area and found that he was playing a match at one of them in a few days. I served him with the subpoena on the golf course and on the first tee. I don't imagine he shot too well that day.

After my retirement from the railroad, an attorney retained me to serve an important summons on an individual who lived in Southern Oregon. Several process servers and other investigators had tried and failed.

I drove to the town in Southern Oregon and spent a couple of days checking around town to see if I could pick up any leads where to find this individual, and wasn't having much luck. Even though the town was small, it appeared that this witness had been swallowed up. The only lead I could develop was that he had married about ten years before in a nearby city. I drove to that town and went straight to the Marriage License Bureau at the county courthouse.

One of the two ladies in the office asked if she could help me and I told her I wanted a marriage license. She said, "For whom?" I said, "For myself." The other lady smiled and asked where my bride was. I told her that I hadn't found her yet, but when I did, I would be all ready to go if I had a license. Both the ladies laughed and one of them jokingly said, "Would one of us do?" I told them they were both very attractive, but I was pretty particular and wanted to look around some more.

I then became serious and told them I had a difficult job for them. I explained that I was looking for the marriage license of an individual who had been married ten years before. I knew that if they could find the license it would contain the address and names of the parents of the individual I was trying to locate. The parents possibly would know the whereabouts of their son. I told them that I knew they would have to go through old files in the archives or in the basement, but that I needed the license that day. I also told them if they located the license I would take them to lunch at the best restaurant in town. When I came back at noon they had found the license.

I was then able to check with the father in another city who told me that his son was living as a recluse in the hills near another city. He said that he was the only one who knew the whereabouts of his son and that I was lucky I had contacted him. The father accompanied me to the run down home where his son was living with other "flower children" and I was able to serve the subpoena. In this case the man wanted to be a trial witness so there wasn't a problem.

After I had worked in Kansas City for six years, I was asked to work in the main Omaha office in a higher paying position. There was a top troubleshooter from the Omaha office who would come to Kansas City now and then. This fellow was a great guy but he was very thrifty with money. He would call me and say, "I will be in Kansas City tomorrow and I am buying the coffee." This was a signal for me to find a place where I could get coffee for twenty-five cents instead of thirty-five cents. I would check all the area restaurants until I found one that served coffee for the lower price. This fellow told me that a promotion was coming up in the home office and I was the leading candidate for the job.

Even though I would have had a bigger title and an increase in salary, I would have been a small fry in the Omaha office. Headquarters had all kinds of senior officials managing the railroad's 25,000 employees. I felt that it was much better to be a big fish in a little pond than a small fish in a big pond. Furthermore, I enjoyed working as an investigator. I loved making direct contact with people. The new management position would have had me supervising other investigators and advising them on tough decisions.

In any event, when I was approached about the promotion to Omaha I told the fellow who liked twenty-five cent coffee that although I appreciated being considered for the job, that I was like him. He asked me what I meant and I told him that I was like him in that money wasn't everything. He liked the answer and said he would see what he could do about getting me back to the West Coast.

It was not that easy to turn down a promotion to the corporate headquarters in Omaha, but I did. Instead, I told them I wanted to return to the Northwest. I had been away from Oregon for twelve years and I was eager to get back to family and friends. My children were growing older and I wanted them to become better acquainted with their grandparents. I was ready to spend the rest of my working career in the Northwest and, shortly thereafter, my railroad career came full circle. I was transferred back to Portland as Assistant Manager of Claims of the Northwest Territory.

Before I left Kansas City, a railroad worker called me for a luncheon date saying he said he had something important to discuss with me. At lunch he told me he was in trouble and wanted me to help straighten out his problem by talking to his very upset girlfriend, who I knew slightly.

It seems his girlfriend had been out of town recently and on that particular night there had been storm warnings about a possible tornado on its way. His girlfriend's best friend called, said she was home alone and was very scared about the coming storm. She suggested that he come over and keep her company. He went over to allay her fear about the storm, but when he got to her house, she had a bottle of liquor with the mixes ready, and immediately suggested they have a drink to brace up for the storm.

The storm was delayed, and after they each had a couple of drinks she suggested that they go to her bedroom to look at the new bed she had just bought. When they got to the bedroom she invited him to sit and bounce on the bed with her to see how soft the mattress was. He bounced up and down and the next thing he knew he was in bed with her. Much later, after a romantic session, she said, "George, how did this ever happen to us. I guess the tension from the storm (which never arrived) was why you couldn't control yourself." George told me the real storm came when she told his girlfriend how *he* had seduced *her*. I told George I would talk to his girlfriend but, before I could do that, she made up with him.

We finally returned to the Northwest after a six-year tour of duty in Kansas City. We would certainly miss our friends and the people of Kansas City, but not the weather. I remember shoveling snow from my driveway almost every single morning for weeks.

I worked primarily out of Portland and Seattle in my new territory, and was required to spend a great deal of time away from home during the week. I was lucky to be home on the weekends.

Occasionally I took Vallen, a friend and a terminal superintendent at the Seattle Railroad yard, along when I was working in the Seattle area. If he was not busy and after checking the yard, he enjoyed going with me when I interviewed witnesses. At times I used him to witness signatures, etc. He always remained in the background while I did my work.

I had an important witness to contact on a serious case. Val and I drove to her address and while we were in the living room taking her statement, her husband walked in. He became furious as soon as he saw us, and yelled, "How dare you come into our home and have business with my wife when I am not at home." I wondered how in the world I was going to finish this woman's crucially important statement. I knew an apology would be of little value, and decided that a string of white lies was in order. I immediately turned to Val (who was taking all of this in and wondering how I was going to get out of it), shook my finger at him and said, "You see there. You see there. I told you we should have contacted her husband but, oh no, you were so right. You're always so right. You have to have it your own way. Well, I certainly hope you are satisfied now." Of course, all Val did was to blink his eyes in dismay. After all, he didn't have anything to do with it except as a spectator. The husband seemed quite pleased after I finished my tirade on Val. He ordered Val to leave the house, turned to me and told me to finish my business. As I was leaving he said that I was welcome anytime, but never to bring "that other guy."

Val had a good sense of humor. When I got back to the car he said this was the first time he really got roasted and toasted for saying and doing absolutely nothing. He said I almost had him convinced that he actually did something wrong. I apologized and announced that dinner was on me.

Val is deceased now. He was a great person and a good friend, notwithstanding my having put him on the hot seat on that occasion.

It was my custom not to call first, but to make cold calls on witnesses. I discovered that when I called witnesses on the telephone they were usually not all that interested in giving me a statement and would come up with any excuse not to see me.

Upon contacting one lady at her apartment, she immediately suggested we meet at a nearby restaurant to discuss the accident. She said there would be big trouble if her boyfriend found us together in their apartment—no matter what my business was. We went to the restaurant and I arranged to take her statement at a table in full view of the large windows overlooking the sidewalk and street.

I investigated a very sad double fatality case. A lady was picking berries alongside the track when she heard the train whistle blow. She saw the train heading straight for her small grandson who was standing in the middle of the track near a curve and made a desperate run to save him. Unfortunately, the train struck and killed them both. Cases like this one cannot help but place the train engineer and the investigator in a sad state of mind for a long time. It is so difficult to time a call on the family after an accident of this type. If an investigator calls on the family too soon, it can give the impression that the railroad is pushing the case, is not respecting the survivors, and allowing them time to go through the grieving process. If the investigator permits too much time to pass without making contact, it may seem the railroad doesn't give a damn about the accident. I usually called a relative or close neighbor of the family and explained that—although I wanted to speak with the family—I wanted above all to respect their grief and could the neighbor or relative let me know when would be an appropriate time for me to make contact.

I was working the Seattle Territory during the 1962 World's Fair. Our trains were filled bringing people from all over the country to Seattle for the fair. Union Station at Seattle had an escalator from the main lobby to the train station platform below of about fifty moving steps.

One day, a lady was riding the escalator. For some unknown reason, she tumbled backward right before she stepped onto the solid platform at the top of the escalator. This rather hefty woman went down those steps like a bowling ball and ended up taking most of the other people on the escalator with her. People were stacked all over like bowling pins in an alley at the bottom of the escalator. That single incident alone kept me busy for several weeks.

I was in the train station lobby one day when a band of drunk and rough-looking individuals came sauntering through. They started to overturn vases and shrubs and were creating quite a disturbance. A city policeman and

his companion were in the lobby at the time and the policeman remarked that if they stopped the toughest looking one
of the bunch the others would probably simmer down. After
quite a struggle, the policeman's companion finally got the
"pick of the litter" in a chokehold and asked the policeman to
hit the fellow over the head with his nightstick. The policeman said he just couldn't do that after which his companion
replied, "Okay. You hold him and I'll do it." This wasn't done,
of course, but the strategy finally worked and things calmed
down.

I was involved in a similar incident. I had worked a case
out of town and flew back into Portland late at night. I took
the airport bus to a hotel about a block from my office. As I
was leaving the hotel area, I noticed a great deal of broken
glass and saw that a number of sidewalk planters had been
knocked over. When I was about a half a block from my office I saw three young hooligans kicking and destroying any
object they could find. Obviously, they had been drinking or
were on drugs. When they saw me, they started towards me.
Fortunately, a police squad car arrived about that time.

As the two policemen were getting out of the car, one of
them was attacked without warning and kicked in the groin
by one of the young men. The policeman's legs buckled under him. When the violator came at him again, the officer
stepped to the side and knocked the man down with his fist. I
was an observer to the whole incident until other policemen
arrived.

It was about this time that a middle-aged man came rushing over to me. Apparently, he was the father of one of the
young toughs. He asked me if I had seen his son being bru-
tally punched by the policeman. He asked for my name and
telephone number. I told him that I had absolutely seen everything and would be willing to testify, especially about when
the policeman was kicked in the groin. As the man strode
away, grumbling under his breath, I went over to the officer

who had received the blow and gave him my card should he need a witness.

Built around the turn of the century, the "Spokane" was a business car used by officials of the Spokane International Railroad. All of its interior woodwork, turn-of-the-century cabinetry and furnishings were absolutely magnificent. The car had polished oak paneling in the interior and brass grillwork on the platform. It had sleeping accommodations for fifteen employees. It also had two staterooms and a lounge. It is rumored that in "the old days" of the railroad the "Spokane" had been a haven for the officials of the Spokane International Railroad. They would park the car on a siding near a lake and fish from the car's vestibule.

A congenial, successful shopping-center developer bought the "Spokane." He intended to bring the car from Spokane to Seattle and use it to entertain guests. The car left Spokane on the Union Pacific for Seattle and the new owner and his friends made plans to meet the car in Seattle when it arrived. In order to ensure that the car's interior would be comfortable for the its greeters in Seattle, it was decided to turn the steam on in Tacoma. When the car was spotted on a track in Tacoma, an employee from another railroad hooked on a steam hose to the car. Unfortunately, the hose he connected contained 120 lbs. of pressure steam and it was fastened to a hose from a car that could only handle 60 lbs. of steam. This caused the hose inside the car to burst and spread an immense amount of hot steam inside the car. The employee walked away thinking the car would be satisfactorily heated. Well, it certainly was and more so—the steam simply destroyed the interior of the car. Among other things, all the beautiful wooden cabinetry became unglued. It was impossible to restore the car to its original state. John Erlichman, later President Nixon's aid, was the businessman's attorney and the case was tried in Seattle. The case was ultimately settled for a business car.

I investigated a case where a man sustained injuries when he fell off a flat car loaded with scrap metal. I went to the metal plant to obtain additional information and was given the name and address of a crane operator who supposedly witnessed the accident. Because I had to be in Portland the following day for a trial, I went to his address that night.

His run-down house was in a rough part of town and there were no lights on when I pulled up in front. I was disappointed because I thought no one was home, but I went to the door and knocked anyway—just in case. Much to my surprise, the door opened and I found myself facing a huge man blocking the doorway. I asked him if his name was Jones and, after he answered, "Yes," I told him I wanted to talk to him about the accident he may have witnessed at the metal plant.

He invited me in and apologized for the electrical problems. I followed his huge frame into a dimly lit kitchen, the only light being from a Coleman camping lantern on the kitchen table. I noticed four things in the kitchen right away—two butcher knives and a bottle of wine on the drainboard and another giant of a man sitting at the table. I couldn't tell if the two men had been drinking, but they appeared sober.

The man who invited me in, introduced me to his friend, Amos. We shook hands and I proceeded to obtain Mr. Jones' statement on the typewriter I carried with me.

The trouble began when I handed the long statement to Mr. Jones to read and sign. He took the statement over to the Coleman lantern, looked at it and then turned to me and told me he could not read. Amos volunteered that he could read and write and I suggested that perhaps he could read the statement for him.

Amos began to read the statement. It went something like this: "It says here…a statement of Elmer Jones. Now, that is correct because that is your name. Age forty-two.

Man, is you forty-two? You told me you was thirty-eight and you told Lucy the other day you was only thirty-two. Residing at 1440 Clinton Street. Now, that is correct. I know the address here. Single. You should have told him how many times you has been married. Now, pays attention to what I am reading because this is very important. You may have to go to court on this." Amos continued, "It says here...I worked for the metal plant for five years." Then he added, "Has it been that long? You should have put in there that it was my brother that got you the job." Amos continued reading on through the statement, adding a personal comment after each sentence.

I could see this was really irritating Mr. Jones and was about to interrupt, when Mr. Jones spoke up in a surly voice and said, "Look here, Amos. You don't have to act so damn smart just because you can read and write and I can't." Amos countered with, "What in the hell is the matter with you? Man, I am doing this for your benefit." This exchange was followed by rougher remarks by both men after which the two huge men actually started shoving each other around towards the counter and those two knives. It appeared the entire situation was going to turn violent, so I stepped in between the two of them—almost getting clipped by a fist thrown by Mr. Jones at Amos. There was a brief pause, after which I said, "Look here, you two. You fellows have been very nice to me. You are both good people and I would really feel bad if you got into a fight. That would not help anybody. Please, Amos. Just read the statement and don't make any comments. I really appreciate how you are both helping me to do my job."

Both men settled down after this. I had Amos sign a statement advising that he had read the statement to Mr. Jones who said it was true and correct. I then visited with them for a short while to continue to cool them down. They wanted me to stay longer and have a glass of wine with them, but I politely refused telling them I was still on duty and took my leave with a big sigh of relief. When I got out in the street I could hear the two men arguing again. There was no way I was going to stick around, but I often wonder what happened after I left.

Taking statements on a typewriter is a large part of an investigator's work. These statements are somewhat like a small deposition in that they state all the history of an individual and the facts of the accident or incident. After I retired from the railroad and was working for private attorneys, an opposing attorney questioned me at a trial as to how many statements I had taken during my investigative career. I testified that my best estimate would be about 15,000—20,000. When I first started as an investigator I would take as many as three to five statements each day. This number was drastically reduced when I became a supervisor.

Statements were not short—some ran two or three pages on legal-size paper, single-spaced. The length of the statement depended on the seriousness of the accident or incident. One I recall, in particular, ran five solid pages.

The fastest statement taker I ever knew was a man who worked for the Milwaukee Road. He could type as fast as a person could talk and not miss a beat. Now, you have to remember this was before computers. Egads, this was even before electric typewriters. These statements were taken on manual typewriters and there were no correction keys. We just typed as fast and as accurately as we could. I am still doing that right now.

When I began working for private attorneys, I always gave them the following dialogue the first time I met them. "I know this is not necessary to say as far as you are concerned but, I want it to go on the record that I will do my best to obtain the true facts of the accident or incident. If the ball bounces bad for you as to the facts, that's going to be your problem—not mine." I cannot remember one single attorney who said he wanted it any other way.

Toward the end of my railroad career, I taught an investigating class to young investigators through the American Association of Railroads. I always emphasized the importance of taking statements exactly as given by the witness. Only a small number of investigators will not do this. They are more interested in getting the facts to agree with what is best for their side of the case than in the truth. If they do fudge on the facts, it may very well come back to bite them. It's never helpful when a witness testifies in court and contradicts the statement he gave the investigator, or testifies that he was coached by the investigator to state things in a particular way. I always pointed out to the students in my classes that they were not lawyers; that their job was to obtain the true facts for them.

On one occasion I was using an interpreter to secure a statement from a young Spanish man. The interpreter was quite an attractive young lady. I suggested she begin the interview by asking the young man his age and whether he was married. This was followed with about a five-minute conversation between just the two of them. Finally, she simply told me that he was twenty-two years old and single. Out of curiosity I asked her, "Why the long conversation for two simple questions?" She said, "Oh, he was telling me about almost being married on three occasions. Then he asked me for a date and I told him that I had a boyfriend, but that I would keep him in mind because he was so cute."

Sometimes witnesses would tell me they didn't want to give a statement because they didn't want to get involved. I would simply tell them that they were already involved because their name was on the police report or appeared in some other documentation relative to the case. I explained that it was unlikely that either side would attempt any settlement without getting the true facts from all the witnesses. Generally, I ended up getting the statement I needed.

I have taken statements in all kinds of places—my car, on a train, on a bus...just about anywhere I could set my lil'

A cooperative witness.
He suggested that I use his grease rack for a table instead of placing
the typewriter on my lap to type his statement. (1988)

ol' typewriter down. I don't know how many times I sat on
a chair with my typewriter balanced on my lap. Once I was
in a garage where the only piece of furniture was a chair.
The owner of the garage lowered the auto hoist down to
table level, and I took the man's statement while I sat in the
chair and the typewriter rested on the auto hoist.

I would have a difficult time typing when little kids
were around. They always wanted to come over and place
their hands on the typewriter. I remember one time in particular, when I was sitting on a sofa with the typewriter on
my lap taking a woman's statement. One of her small children was lying on the top of the sofa and on my shoulder.
His younger brother was seated beside me poking the typewriter keys with his fingers as I was trying to type. The
mother would say, "Jimmy! Johnny! Get away from the man.

Don't bother him." The two children would move away for a moment or two, and then move right back in and pick up where they left off. Children simply found the clicking of the typewriter keys, the clang of the margin bell and the sound of the carriage return irresistible. I battled to keep cheerful in situations like that. I would have liked to be able to tell those kids, "Get off my back and get away from me; can't you see I'm busy." But then I don't think I would have gotten the statement had I done that. What we had to put up with at times to get the job done! An investigator has to remember that the witness is helping you—you are not helping them. And there isn't anything on the books that they are required to give you a statement.

I was sitting on a rail in the desert east of The Dalles interviewing a track laborer. As I was typing, I just happened to glance to my right and there, about six feet away, was a rattlesnake curled up inside the rail. Snakes like the warmth of the rail, particularly on a sunny day. This rattlesnake was not very large so I felt it would be safe to move a short distance away. Apparently, the snake liked the click-click noise of the typewriter. Perhaps it sounded like a rattle. I also noticed that it cocked its head toward me every time the margin bell would ding. In any event, I wanted it to keep its nose out of my investigation, so I moved.

It was always interesting taking an individual's statements. Some people would barely furnish any information, while others wouldn't stop talking. I was with a claims investigator of another railroad while he was taking the statement of a witness. This person had seen a cow getting struck by an automobile injuring the occupants on railroad property. The witness not only talked about the accident, but also kept talking and talking about the history of cows. I can still see the claims man impatiently snapping his suspenders for a long time waiting at his typewriter for the witness to finish his lecture on cows. The man proudly informed us that he was a historian on cows and the claims man had to separate the facts of the accident from the history of cows and how much milk each breed of cow could give.

When working for Frem Nielsen in Spokane, I had to obtain a statement from a lady who was a key witness in a serious death case. I called at her home in a small town in Eastern Washington. She was of the tugboat Annie type, and when entering her home to obtain a statement, I was met with an over-whelming odor. The lady had about ten cats, four dogs, and a room full of birds in cages. I had no choice but to proceed taking her statement while seated on a sofa. As I was typing, several dogs were trying to lick my hands and face along with nuzzling my sides. The cats were purring and rubbing against my ankles. After typing for only a few minutes, the smell was so offensive I told the lady I was not feeling well from an upset stomach; that it was necessary for me to go outside for some fresh air. I would then return to the house after being outside for about five minutes. This was repeated approximately three times during my stay. Upon my departure, the lady remarked that I was looking pale, also I should see a doctor for a check-up. It flashed through my mind I should tell her that she should check with a veterinarian and learn how to tidy up on pets. Instead I smiled and thanked her for her concern.

Several days later when talking with Frem, I told him about the difficulty I had when obtaining the statement. He immediately joked and said the statement certainly did not cover the waterfront, also I should go back and obtain a far more lengthy statement. I told Frem this would be fine is someone furnished me an oxygen mask.

Although in later years with the railroad I used recorders when taking statements over the telephone, I believe visiting with the witness one-on-one and using a typewriter ("the old-fashioned way") produces a superior product. The latter provides the investigator an opportunity to evaluate the witness and have him draw sketches of the accident area. Also, on many occasions, the witness will give you information "off the record" which they would not have provided over the telephone, or if a recorder is in sight. Once the information is recorded it is etched in stone. Carl Hawker and Ray McDeid, two ace investigators, retired from the railroad and now work with attorneys providing investigative services. They take typewritten (laptop computer) statements and both are very successful.

People can be strange and puzzling. You never know what you might run into while in their homes. A man I attempted to contact for a statement was not home. A neighbor told me that he and his three young teenaged daughters were out picketing an area where a businessman was contemplating putting in a nude bar. I went back to the home later that evening and while in their living room I saw their picket signs containing phrases like "No Nudity Wanted—We Want Decency." The three young girls were listening to the television while I was taking their father's statement. They made no effort to turn the television down so I could not help but hear part of the program. Imagine my surprise when I realized these girls were watching a drama where a woman was seducing a man into bed displaying all kinds of nudity. What a contradiction these people were living. They didn't give a second thought about inviting nudity into their living room, but were willing to go to great lengths to see that it wasn't allowed down the street with the door closed.

Taking statements can also be humorous. One evening Don Toman, another investigator for the railroad, and I had to contact members of a motorcycle gang in a rough neighborhood of Tacoma. Although the men we interviewed were certainly a rough looking lot, they treated us quite nicely and gave us the statements we needed. We had entered their home through the kitchen, but when it came time for us to leave, we exited through the back porch. It was very dark in that place and when I said my last goodbye, I turned around to find Don missing. I was really perplexed because just a moment before he had been standing right behind me. When I called his name, Don yelled back that he had just fallen off the deck. It seems the bikers had been putting in concrete steps at the end of the porch that day and they had only gotten as far as placing sand at the bottom of the porch. Well, there was Don sprawled in the sand pile about five feet down. He yelled, "Lou, I'm down here! Watch that first step. It's a doozy and it certainly isn't a first step for mankind."

Normally, after taking a statement I would take a little extra time and engage a witness in conversation that didn't relate to the accident. I met a number of memorable and very interesting people over the years in this manner.

I contacted a darling elderly lady in a small Mid-West city near Chicago. She had taught public school for nearly fifty years and had recently retired. I was looking for information about a former student who had gone mentally berserk. She told me that as a youngster he definitely had problems, but so did his parents. They flaunted authority, refused to believe their son needed help and considered themselves free thinkers.

I had about an hour to kill before I had to catch a train so the lady and I settled in and had a most wonderful chat. I asked her of all the students she ever taught, which group was the most successful in later life. She replied that it was not the "whiz" kids or the "poor" students, but the students who got good grades by working hard to keep their grades up. They were the ones who got a lot of personal satisfaction out of their accomplishments. Surprisingly, they were the ones who would come back and visit her after they graduated and in later life. To her, they seemed the most happy and contented.

She thought that too many people were just "working for the money" and working jobs they didn't particularly like. She felt, and rightly so in my book, that that was such a sad waste of one's life. She also pointed out that people who usually do not like their jobs do not contribute to a positive environment.

She believed there was too much laxity in our school system, which reflected poorly on the home environment. She stressed that as adults we have to live by certain rules—that we can't go down the freeways at any speed we want, or break rules and laws that result in unfavorable consequences for ourselves and for society. She was saddened that youngsters were not being taught this way from a very young age. Amazingly, she thought the problem would undoubtedly become a lot worse if something wasn't done to correct it. I don't know if this lady is still alive—she would be over one hundred years old now—but I don't think she would be too surprised that some of our schools find it necessary to hire guards.

Another prophetic point she made concerned attire. She said when someone dresses in a drastic or odd manner to flaunt or to get attention, it provokes ridicule and harassment from other students. This quickly builds bridges that can lead to hatred. She faulted the elimination of dress codes in the seventies.

I thought of her words when I heard of the unfortunate killings at a high school in Littleton, Colorado. The killers wore long black trench coats and sunglasses to school every day, and were ostracized by the other students.

I found her views so interesting that I almost missed my train. Later, when I returned to my office, I sent her a thank-you card for assisting me in my investigation and for the interesting conversation.

Perhaps I have a phobia about how one is dressed. I dislike seeing people wearing shorts to church. I guess this is something that goes way back in my life when people dressed up for special occasions. All through my thirty-six years with Union Pacific and the twenty years I worked for private attorneys, I always wore a tie with a sport coat or suit.

Recently, an investigator I'd never met before called and asked to meet with me. He wanted to discuss "joining forces" because he was aware I had a lot of work, and he didn't. This revelation rather surprised me, because I had heard he was quite capable. At the time I talked with him he was wearing a white underwear T-shirt and a black leather jacket. Investigators on television dress in that fashion, but in real life, an investigator should be well dressed when he calls on a witness (male or female) and when talking to attorneys. I told the investigator, in a nice way, that the appearance of an investigator was important, and that his look, in my opinion, was a detriment and a possible sign that he was not a professional. We talked on other matters, and the next time we met he told me that his caseload had increased. He was wearing a nice suit, and he had a highly improved attitude.

I have a very high regard for sectionmen—called railroad track workers in my early days with the railroad. They perform manual labor in all kinds of weather. One morning I was leaving The Dalles for my office in Portland, and took the Columbia River Highway (I-84) that runs along the Columbia River. It was bitter cold and the cutting easterly winds were howling through the gorge. I passed several men working the rails on the edge of the river with the cold wind snapping at them. I felt sorry for them so I turned around and drove back to The Dalles where I purchased hot coffee and doughnuts. I drove back to where the gang was working and brought them my purchase.

The old saying that, "What goes around comes around," I found to be true, when several years later this same gang was involved in an accident. I was pleased when the men said they preferred to discuss the accident with me, rather than with some of the other outside supervisors.

I give credit where credit is due, and I want to recognize the hard work of railroad workers. Think of the brakemen who switch boxcars all night in the railroad yard—walking and running to throw switches in the snow and rain. Enginemen have to be sharp and alert sitting in the cab of 600-ton power engines pulling 150 cars. Too much or too

When inpsecting a railroad yard , I ran into the above.
The coupling of an engine against this string of cars at either end
would have been disasterous to the trespassers.

little throttle could result in damage to the wheels of cars or
slack action also resulting in injuries.

We should also recognize the members of the families
of railroad workers who have to put up with the absence of
their loved ones, especially on weekends and holidays.

I was promoted to District Claim Agent of the Northwest Territory in 1972. There were five investigators and
one secretary in the territory who were responsible for handling all the claim work in Oregon, Washington and Idaho.
My major role was now to supervise and help other investigators with their problems in their territories. I was also
required to work more directly with the Operating and
Safety Departments of the railroad, and be more involved
with attorneys in disputed claims and trials. Unfortunately,
my new position nearly eliminated my working directly
with claimants—something I enjoyed immensely. Once in
a while, however, I still found myself working one-on-one

with someone who had an odd or unusual claim against the railroad.

I was in my office one morning when a handsome bearded giant of a man weighing about 350 lbs. and around six-foot-seven came into our front office and in a loud voice asked our secretary, "Who in the hell is running this joint?" She pointed at my door. Without another word, he pushed open the door and walked over to the window in my office. Looking out the window, the first words out of his mouth were, "How many floors is it to the street?" "Eight," I replied. I wasn't exactly comforted by his next choice of words—"Well," he said, "I am going to throw you out of this window and see how far you bounce after you hit the street." That was quite a wild threat. I pointed to a chair and told him to sit down, and we would talk. It turned out that this man and his followers had a grievance against another company—not the railroad. After I had quieted him down, I invited him down to the small *ground floor* coffee shop in our building, and treated him to a cup of coffee. In the meantime, one of my investigators was sent to confirm the facts I had provided the huge man. He took a sip of his coffee, and said that he had never found a restaurant that could make good coffee. He explained his recipe for making a great cup of coffee: "Mix the coffee grounds, the milk and the water together and boil all three at the same time." Somehow, I don't think Starbuck's has anything to worry about.

My friends in the coffee shop kidded me about my Jolly Green Giant coffee partner, and that night's news carried a story about him and his followers picketing a company in the area. I was certainly glad that he didn't picket Union Pacific on television before talking to us.

Speaking of powerful physical men—I now have breakfast with a group of businessmen almost every morning. I grew up with these influential men, and we sit together and discuss, among other things, politics and local news. One morning a huge and handsome man walked into the restaurant. His name is Stan Brock and he played offensive guard for many years for the San Diego Chargers. He must have weighed at least 275 pounds and all of it pure muscle. One of the men in our group introduced him around the breakfast table. After we shook hands, I said to him, "You know, when you walked in I was thinking of inviting you outside, but you seem to be a real nice guy so I changed my mind." (I am almost eighty years old and walking with a cane.) Without batting an eyelash he jokingly said, "Thanks a lot for letting me off the hook." He's a sharp guy who now coaches a professional football team.

I was conducting a lot of my work by phone, and one day I received a telephone call from Melvin Belli, the famous attorney who defended Jack Ruby. Mr. Belli asked me how much we were going to pay on a serious accident case. I told him, "Nothing at this time." My response startled him and he asked me why we were not making an offer. I told him that I thought he had counseled in one of his books: "On occasion do not settle with some insurance company (or railroad) until you get on the courthouse steps." I told Mr. Belli that we were about six months from trial and asked him why he thought we should make an offer if it didn't have a chance of being accepted. Mr. Belli then came back and said, "Oh, you read my book." I told him that I had found it good reading. He wanted to know if I had read his latest book. When I told him I hadn't, he said he would send me a copy. True to his word, a personally autographed copy of his book arrived. After I retired, I sent him a small box of Love apples. He thanked me for the apples, and invited me to stop in and see him whenever I was in San Francisco.

I had an excellent secretary in the Portland office named Jeanine. One day she told me that she was going to Seattle just to look around the city on a mini-vacation. I mentioned to Jim, our Seattle investigator, that Jeanine was coming to his area, and suggested he take her to a nice dinner along one of the lakes. Jim had talked to Jeanine on the telephone almost every morning for some time, but had never met her. He thought the dinner idea was a good one and made arrangements to meet her in Seattle. Well, when Jeanine got back from her trip she just raved about the nice treatment she received from Jim—that he had taken her to a beautiful restaurant on a lake, and that he was a delightful host. Six months passed and Jeanine, my very capable secretary, came into my office and announced that she was leaving us, moving to Seattle and marrying Jim.

This took me by complete surprise. Although she had discussed a few personal things with me, she had never mentioned having a steady boyfriend. Thinking back, I should have known it was Jim. Another investigator had told me that Jim had called on Jeanine at her apartment wearing a brand new suit. Unfortunately, Jeanine's poodle decided to go to the bathroom on the pant leg of Jim's new suit. I guess it didn't *dampen* Jim's enthusiasm for the relationship. They were married shortly thereafter, and I was proud to be the best man.

When Jeanine resigned I had the difficult task of finding someone to replace her. Alice (a young African-American woman with a very nice appearance) worked across the hall from us as a clerk in another department. She was always neatly dressed and seemed to do a good job. I thought she would be an asset to our office, and I went to see her supervisor. He gave her a high performance rating and said although he would hate to lose her, he wouldn't stand in her way. He recognized that being promoted from a clerk to an officer was a good career move. I went to Alice and told her there was an opening in my department and offered her the position. She seemed pleased and said that she would check with her husband and get back to me. The following day she said she had talked the matter over with her husband and, although she appreciated being considered for the job, she had to decline. She and her husband had agreed that it would be quite difficult for her to work weekends on emergencies because of their two small children.

The position was still open a week later when two young minority ladies came in to apply for the job. They were very inappropriately dressed to interview for a job in my office because they were both wearing odd shoes with slacks and sweaters. I politely told them they did not fit in with what I was looking for—a big mistake. Several weeks later the Union Pacific Railroad and I were sued for racial discrimination. When I told affable George King, my boss in Omaha, about the lawsuit, he commented, "Well, Lou, let's see how you get out of this one."

About a month after the suit was filed, an investigator from the government came to my office to interview me. I told him the reason I did not want to hire the two young ladies was because of the way they were dressed. I pointed out that we had a very nice office and, as he could see, I wanted someone who would add to it—not detract from it. I then told him that it was absolutely immaterial to me what nationality, color or religion an applicant was, but that it was important to me the individual was one with whom I could be comfortable. I told him I had previously offered the job to Alice. I also told him that I probably should have given them a test and, if they passed, told them what I expected in the way of appearance and dress. I pointed out that it was important to me how a person was dressed when applying for a job. The investigator said he wanted to interview Alice and would get back to me. He returned and said that he was recommending the lawsuit be dropped; that it was obvious to him racial discrimination was not involved.

My tour as district claims manager was made easier because of the very capable investigators who worked with me—Carl Hawker, Jim Olson, Ray McDeid, Jack Pfeifer, Rod Carnahan and Frank Hart. The old saying, "A ship is only as good as its crew," is very true.

Ray McDeid, our Spokane investigator, wrote an article that was published in November of 1979.

It read:

"My family and I hosted Takayuki Nakamura, a 28 year-old Japan National Railroad conductor who was visiting the United States under the Railway Worker's Program, An Experiment in International Living. He is married. His wife is 27 years of age and they have a little boy almost two years of age. Their home is near Takeno, Japan, which is on the Sea of Japan. About 1000 Japanese National workers are selected to take a test each year. Then based upon this test and their work product the company picks only 30 employees for the trips to the United States. They are divided into three touring groups of ten employees each. The trip is paid for by the company and is part of their incentive program. Their tour this year started with two days in San Francisco, then eight days here in Spokane, Washington. They were in Washington D.C., New York City and Los Angeles. Takayuki had to be back to work on November 21. For their stay in Spokane, the workers are placed in homes of American railway workers, preferably, although they stay with others too. By doing so they learn how we live and work, and we in turn also learn from them. The majority of the Japanese workers stayed in homes of Burlington Northern employees, and I was aware of only one other Union Pacific family involved.

Takayuki spoke rather poor English, but he always carried his Japanese-English dictionary. After a few days we were able to communicate better, and I learned that he is a passenger train conductor and his trains work much the same as ours. His train has one engine and about 12 cars with a seating capacity of about 1,000. An average load is about 700 people.

I inquired about employee's personal injuries, passenger injuries and claims. I learned that the government handles the claims and they have a claims investigator and Takayuki said of him, "He is a very tired man." We got quite a laugh out of that. Employees are paid their lost time and passengers are also taken care of. As to grade crossing accidents, I learned they have a very few rail crossings at grade, most are grade separations. At grade crossings in Japan a vehicle must come to a complete stop at each crossing and must yield right-of-way to the trains. He told me his train has never hit a car. We read together the newspaper account of a truck and train accident here in Spokane. He was very interested in the accident and with sadness asked about the employee's families.

Mr. Ruchek was here during the week he was here and he had the pleasure of meeting Takayuki. Shortly after my "boss" left for home, Takayuki asked me about our "de boss weight in American." Well, I was curious why he wanted to know how much Mr. Ruchek weighed, but I didn't question it and just tossed some figure at him. He looked puzzled, then drew a man and a woman in pairs, and asked again about "de boss weigh." After trying twice, he went to the dictionary, and I learned he had been asking me about our "divorce rate" in America. After I had explained about "de boss weigh", we both had a hearty laugh.

Each day of his stay he would pull out a small gift for a member of our family. He was very clean, neat and polite with perfect manners. His favorite meat was a Big Mac at McDonald's. He drank his first beer and said, "I like very much." He had never roasted a hot dog in a bonfire and really liked that. He burned up three of them and ate them all with relish.

It was quite an experience for our family and when we bade him goodbye at the airport at 7:00 in the morning, tears welled up in his eyes and began trickling down his cheeks as he hugged each member of our family saying how thankful he was for the experience of being in our home. He invited us to stay with him and his family if we ever got to Japan, and at our next quarterly staff meeting I have a suggestion for a work incentive plan for our own railroad employees."

One day I received a letter from Oregon Governor Atiyeh's office enclosing a copy of a letter he had received from a lady who lived alongside a railroad yard in a small town. She had written the governor stating that Percy had died as the result of chemical fumes emanating from our small railroad yard and that she would appreciate a full and complete investigation of the matter to determine if the fumes really caused Percy's death. A copy of this letter was also sent to Tom Harrison, a State Chemical Engineer. Tom had previously worked claims with me. I found him to be a darn good worker and very knowledgeable. I telephoned him and suggested we make a joint call on Mrs. Jones. He agreed and together we drove to her home. Mrs. Jones was elderly and when we asked her who Percy was she promptly said, "Wait just a minute. I will get his body." She went to the refrigerator and brought out an object wrapped in wax paper. It turned out that Percy was a goldfish. Seeing how serious she was about Percy's death, we proceeded to ask her questions such as, "How long was it from the time she last saw Percy alive and when she found him deceased?" She solemnly informed us that Percy was okay when she went to bed at night, but the next morning he was floating in his fish bowl. We asked Mrs. Jones how old Percy was and she told us he was about four years old. We pointed out to this nice lady that she must have taken very good care of Percy because four years is considered a long life for a goldfish. Apparently she was satisfied that Percy had died of old age. When we were leaving she insisted that we take Percy with us. We were able, however, to convince her that Governor Atiyeh would most likely agree that Percy should be buried where he had lived his life—at home. We never heard from her again, but we kept our fingers crossed that we wouldn't receive another letter from Governor Atiyeh's office about Percy.

I've had people compare me to "Columbo," Peter Falk's detective character. The Percy episode certainly evidences how my inquisitive nature coupled with my love of talking to people has served me quite well over the years. I recalled talking to a lady witness about her goldfish and asking how long they lived. She told me some of her fish had lived as long as four or five years. This information came back to me when I was talking about Percy's death.

While I was working for Jim Pippin, I had to contact a prisoner at the Oregon State Penitentiary. He had been an Alaskan fisherman and had stabbed a man to death after drinking several beers. After I finished interviewing the prisoner, I returned to Jim and gave him a verbal report of what I had learned from the prisoner. I also told Jim that I spent some time talking to the man about life in prison and found out that he had seven more years to serve. As I was leaving, the man in prison made the following remark, "You know, you seem to be a pretty good guy. Give me your business card and when I get out I will contact you. We can go fishing and have a few beers." Jim then asked me, "Did you give him your card?" I jokingly said, "Of course not. I gave him yours."

One attorney asked me to investigate a case of road rage. A car passed another on the freeway and came dangerously close to the first car when it cut back in. The driver of the first car then proceeded to pass the second car all the while giving him the finger. Next, the two cars were passing each other and using the finger every time they passed. Finally, both cars came to a halt on the side of the freeway. A deputy sheriff told me that by the time he arrived on the scene, the two wives were fighting, the two husbands were fighting and a four-year-old boy was punching a six-year-old girl. He said that because everyone was fighting he had to call for back up.

Me and two very capable telephone operators who took such good care in tracking me. Taken at my retirement party. (1980)

Ray McDeid, Carl Hawker, Louis Ruchek, and now U.S. Senior Federal Court Judge Frem Nielsen (clockwise from top left) get together for a friendly reunion. All worked for Union Pacific for many years. (1999)

FARMING—SECOND PHASE

I worked as a district claim agent for eight years and, although the work was interesting and the pay was good, the fact remained that I sorely missed the direct contact with people. I decided to retire from the railroad when I was sixty. Nearly 250 guests came to my retirement party, and I was honored that it was attended by attorneys from Spokane, Seattle, Omaha and Portland as well as claims people from other railroads and their attorneys. The entire party was hosted by Union Pacific and, needless to say, I was thoroughly roasted throughout the course of the evening. It was a very special night in my life.

Now that I was retired from the railroad I had to decide what to do. My brother and I still owned the small farm on which I was raised and, for the time being, I decided to get away from the busy world of investigations and attorneys and help operate the farm. I knew the physical labor on the farm would be good for me, and that I would enjoy bringing back the memories of my youth. The farm consisted of about 150 Love apple trees and about four acres of rich lake bottomland that consistently grew the best vegetables one could imagine. The first year I planted about 1,000 tomato plants and four long rows of zucchini, sweet corn and beans. I had a beautiful crop of tomatoes but just about harvest time it rained and I lost the whole crop—what farmers have to go through.

The four acres of land were near the center of Beaverton and we were surrounded by shopping centers, apartment houses and housing subdivisions. By this time the population of Beaverton had grown to around 80,000 and we were known throughout the area as the only farm left in Beaverton. I enjoyed working on the farm. I got up at four o'clock in the morning each day and harvested vegetables until the stores opened. Every day I packed up a load of produce and delivered it to nearby stores. It turned out that I was not a very profitable farmer. Expenses were high, and I gave away so much that there was little profit left. Nevertheless, I enjoyed selling the produce to the people from the surrounding apartments and homes. I recall a mother with several children who came to the farm to buy vegetables. She was originally from Africa, and we had many interesting conversations about Africa while her little ones played among the cornstalks.

In order to sell my produce and apples more quickly I contacted my friend, Jack Meek, who owned a lot bordering a busy highway that ran through Beaverton. He gave me permission to park my pickup loaded with vegetables and fruit on the lot to sell directly to the public.

One day I was standing near the busy highway next to my pickup loaded with fruit when a large truck pulled in filled with about a ton and a half of fresh-picked corn. The farmer got out of his truck and asked me if I would permit him to sell his corn alongside my fruit. I told him it would not be a problem, and his corn sold rapidly to the occupants of passing cars. For the next two days he arrived at the lot to sell his corn and was sold out after three-fourths of the day had passed. On about the third or fourth day of this arrangement the farmer's big truck pulled in and parked by mine. Imagine my surprise when a slender beautiful young lady wearing a skimpy top and dungarees that had been cut off quite short hopped out of the big truck. She explained that her father was busy and asked if I minded if she continued selling the family corn on the lot. I told her this would not be a problem, and she put her "Corn-For-Sale" sign next to the highway and stood by it. Now, as I said, she was wearing a real eye-catching outfit on a very good figure and, boy, did she sell the corn! Young men couldn't make U-turns fast enough on the busy highway to buy her corn after they caught a glimpse of her. She sold that truckload of corn in about one-fourth of the time it took for her father to sell it. I don't know that it helped my business that much, but I enjoyed being there a lot more. I also learned a valuable "marketing" tool.

Later that year I learned another valuable lesson about selling a product. After the vegetable season ended, I concentrated on our apple crop that consisted mainly of Love apples. We picked and shipped tons of them to the Orient in the fall. The best of the Love apples went to the Orient, and the seconds (apples with tiny spots) were sold locally. After the original shipment to the Orient we had about a ton of the seconds left. I went to a large store where I was acquainted with the fruit buyer and asked him if he wanted to purchase any Love apples. I priced them at $.20 per pound. He said he had never had them before but would be willing to give them a try. He intended to sell them for $.35 per pound. I quickly brought him 300 lbs. of apples. I was absolutely stunned, and somewhat embarrassed, to hear that he never sold a single apple after he displayed them in the store. Later, I happened to be at a nearby fruit store and mentioned to the owner that I had about a half-ton of Lady or Love apples to sell. He ordered a couple of hundred pounds, telling me he would see what he could do with them—we would discuss price later. I was shocked when he called me a few days later and said he needed more apples, and he would pay me $.75 per pound. He was selling them for $1.50 per pound. I guess the reason the apples didn't originally sell was because the price was so low that people were of the opinion that they weren't much of an apple. The second storeowner also told me that young ladies were purchasing the apples because they could put three or four in their purse, and later eat them for lunch—to keep their weight down. The guy was a real salesman and he bought every apple I had, all the time telling me he wished I had more. I shared this story with a friend of mine. He mentioned that he knew of a product that was not selling at $150, but when priced at $1,500 sold like hotcakes. Now, if that isn't a real sad lesson in salesmanship.

It was in the early 1980s that my wife and I decided to travel to Europe to visit our daughter, an opera singer. We were unable to fly together because I had a business conflict, but we made arrangements to meet in Brussels, Belgium, where my daughter was performing. My wife left for Europe and I followed a few days later.

My flight was a late night flight and one individual was snoring so loudly that several of the passengers lodged complaints with the stewardess. She woke the snoring passenger several times but, unfortunately, it would be only a few moments before he would fall back asleep and resume his horrendous snoring. It was about this time that the passenger sitting next to me called over to the flight attendant and rudely questioned why she could not keep the passenger from snoring and disturbing everyone else. The pretty young woman lost her cool and snapped back with the question, "What do you want me to do? Hit him over the head with a baseball bat?" The passenger started to snap back at her when I spoke up and said that I thought this was an excellent idea. I further suggested that she use one of the complaining passenger's shoes because a baseball bat was not available; that would put the snoring man in a very good position to sue both of them. The complaining passenger did not think this was funny and was about to say something else when other passengers chipped in with remarks in support of the flight attendant. Needless to say, the only person who got much sleep that trip was the man who snored his way to Europe.

I arrived in London, caught another flight to Brussels and registered at a hotel near the center of the city. I tried to sleep, but I had a good case of jet lag, was uncomfortable from the previous rough night, and was also feeling a bit claustrophobic. I was wide-awake at midnight and decided to get up and go for a walk. I thought a bit of night air might do me good. It was about one o'clock and it appeared that everything was closed. After walking a number of blocks in the semi-darkness, I came to a cocktail lounge that was still open. This seemed strange to me at the time because other establishments of a similar nature were closed. I was curious so I peered through the window to see what was going on, and saw what looked like some kind of party. While I was looking through the window two young girls came out of the lounge, saw me and began speaking to me in their own language. I couldn't understand them so I just said, "American." They then motioned for me to stay where I was and went back inside. A minute or two later another young lady came out who spoke English. She asked me what I was doing and I told her I had just arrived that very night from America, that I could not sleep and that I was just out walking around a bit. She explained that they were having a wedding party and invited me to join in the festivities. For the next hour or two I had a ball—dancing to an orchestra, eating and drinking an occasional glass of wine. I was toasted a number of times after which I toasted the bride and groom in English. The young woman who invited me to the party translated my toast. The pretty bride asked me to dance the "Blue Danube Waltz" with her after which she kissed my cheek. The bridegroom (who had enjoyed a number of drinks) also kissed me on the cheek. I was treated like royalty and simply had a most wonderful time. I left a money gift for the couple, and as I was preparing to leave several of the men suggested they would walk me to my hotel. I thanked them for their concern, but told them I would be fine. I was totally relaxed when I got back to my room and slept like a log until it was time to meet my wife. I woke up feeling a lot more comfortable about being in Europe after meeting those kind and generous people at the wedding party. Unfortunately, that feeling was to be a temporary one. My wife, daughter and I were in London in December of 1983. My wife and daughter wanted to spend the morning shopping at Harrod's Department Store. Harrod's is one of the finest department stores in the world. It's one of those stores that has it if you want it. It even has dog kennels where people can leave their dogs while they shop. I wasn't as enthusiastic as my wife and daughter about spending the morning shopping, so we arranged to meet on a corner outside the store at one o'clock in the afternoon. They were about twenty minutes late. Considering what happened next, it's one of the few times I didn't complain too much.

After meeting at the corner, we proceeded to walk to a store entrance. I was behind them looking at the window displays when I saw a beautiful man's camel hair overcoat and stopped to look at it. My wife and daughter were about fifty feet ahead of me so I decided to catch up. When we were about seventy-five feet into the store, there was a blast that shook the floor underneath our feet and ripped through four floors of the block-long structure. The walls shook and splintered glass flew in all directions—some of which landed only a few feet behind us. The British police suspected the Irish Republican Army had set off the bomb. We had passed the car containing the bomb only a few seconds before, and came that close to being in the carnage that resulted from the explosion. The final tally was five killed and nearly one hundred injured. We were detained in the store for about ten minutes after which we were asked to leave.

I'll never forget the sight of the dead and injured people and the dead police dogs strewn in the street. Apparently, just a few minutes before the blast a man who claimed he was with the IRA phoned the police with a suicide message and warning about the bomb. The police rushed to Harrod's but, unfortunately, were unable to get there in time to prevent the explosion; the terrorists were long gone. It was estimated that the bomb weighed over fifty pounds and had been set off by remote control—possibly from a nearby building. I walked by the window where the camel hair coat had been on display. The coat was still on the mannequin, but it looked as if someone had taken a knife and cut it into shreds. In my confused state, I could only think—I should have purchased the coat before it was ruined.

After I got about fifty feet from the blast area a worldwide television news crew stopped me. The reporter asked me where I was at the time of the explosion, and asked me for my name and address. Upon hearing that I was from the United States he asked, "What do you think of the Irish people now?" Although I was still in shock somewhat, I told him that even as terrible as this whole event was, I could not blame the entire Irish nation for the brutal act of a few people. I never made the news. I can't help but think, however, that had I answered his question differently I would have been seeing myself later on the "tele." It was a most horrible experience and I'm very grateful that we were spared any injury. An estimated 20,000 people were inside Harrod's at the time of the blast, and I'm certain they were ever so thankful too.

We stayed with our daughter in Stuttgart over the 1983 Christmas holidays. While we were there she sent me to a wine shop to pick up a bottle of wine. She told me to catch a bus called "Doggenburg" and it would take me to the wine shop. With a name like that, I didn't have any problem remembering which bus to catch.

I entered the wine shop and gave my daughter's name to the owner. He smiled and brought me the bottle of wine she ordered. I was about to leave when he hand signaled me to a back room that was filled with a generous supply of wine. He proceeded to open a bottle which, by his sign language, he had made. He poured a whiskey glass of wine from that bottle and then poured another glass from a labeled wine. He motioned with his hands for me to drink both glasses and then tell him which one I liked best. I drank both and, of course, I pointed to his wine as being the better of the two. He smiled broadly and repeated the process by using another brand of labeled wine. Again, I pointed to the wine he had made. He was thrilled. He continued this tasting test for some time, and each time I would point to his bottle after which he would grab another brand of wine with a label. This kept up until I got to the point where I could not tell the difference. By this time, I almost pointed to his wine before making the test on another as it really didn't make any difference after so many tests. Although I wanted to continue to please him,—enough was enough—and it was time for me to catch "Dogburger." He was disappointed that I wanted to stop as he had many other bottles of labeled wine to be tested but, as a gift, he gave me a bottle of his own brand to take home with me. I thanked him, left his shop and asked the first German pedestrian I could find where I could catch "Dogburger." She just smiled, pointed and I was on my way. Later, when serving the shop owner's wine at dinner, my daughter asked me where I had gotten the "horrible wine." I simply rolled my eyes up at the ceiling and told her it was a bottle I had picked out by myself. She said it was a very poor choice. I thought I had "better let sleeping dogs lie" and I didn't say anything more.

During our Germany stay my daughter and her German opera colleagues took my wife and me to the Stuttgart opera. After the opera we went to a fashionable restaurant, as it was customary to eat after performances. I told the group at dinner that I had retired from the railroad and was looking for a second career. The gentleman sitting next to me spoke a little English and I asked him if he thought it was possible I could be an opera performer. He failed to catch the humor of this question and answered with some degree of kindness he supposed it was possible.

The next night we went to a ballet with the same German group. Stuttgart has some of the finest ballets in the world. After the performance we again dined with them at a very nice restaurant. I made the remark to the same gentleman that I had talked to the previous night that I had a problem. He was concerned and asked me what was wrong. I then proceeded to tell him the night before we had gone to an opera and I thought I would possibly start a career in opera when I retired from the railroad after forty years. Now, however, after going to such a wonderful ballet I couldn't decide if I should be an opera singer or a ballet dancer for my second career.

By this time, my daughter was nudging me under the table. In any event, the German gentleman answered in a very serious manner, "You do have a problem." In looking back now, I think he meant that in more ways than one. Later, when my wife and I were alone, she jokingly said she could just picture me in a leotard attempting to leap through the air doing a *Tour Jete'*.

Operas and concerts are very popular in Europe, and a lot of musicians and artists from the United States and other countries perform there. The German government subsidizes its operas and Germany alone has about sixty opera houses offering performances every night.

The concert we attended had three choirs containing about 150 individuals each—one choir was comprised of youngsters up to fourteen years of age, one choir had only women and another choir contained only men.

These groups would practice for a period of months after which the main soloists would come in and rehearse with them on one or two occasions. After that, the concert would be performed for the public. On several occasions we had breakfast with two of the soloists—one was from England and the other from Finland. It was enjoyable and quite interesting to talk with them about their background.

We traveled from city to city with the soloists and while they rehearsed we went sightseeing. In the evening we would watch the performances.

We attended a party hosted by one of the leading banks in Brussels after the concert's closing performance. The fare consisted of many delicacies, including boiled pigeon eggs. I met a nice elderly lady, a countess, at the party. She told me her family had owned a ham factory for 300 years. She employed 500 people and their specialty product was canned ham.

Overall, we immensely enjoyed the time we spent in Europe. We were impressed with the giant museum in Munich, and I would recommend this as a "must see" when in Germany.

Shortly after returning from Europe I received a telephone call from a Chinese friend who owned a restaurant in the Beaverton area. He was acquainted with me more or less as an occasional customer and as an investigator who worked with attorneys. He had a parking problem involving his restaurant customers. Apparently, the owner of the property wanted to eliminate some of his parking spaces. I referred him to a capable attorney by the name of Austin Crowe for whom I had worked on previous occasions. Austin handled the problem much to the satisfaction of my Chinese friend and from then on when one of his friends who owned restaurants had a problem they would call me. If the problem was not a legal one, I would handle it. If the problem required an attorney, I would suggest the names of one, two or three attorneys to contact. This relationship grew to where owners of the Chinese restaurants would refer all kinds of problems to me, including murder. This help also extended to their employees. I once referred a waitress to an attorney when she was accused of beating up her boyfriend and charged with assault. The waitress was pleased when the judge threw the case out of court.

I became a good friend of Paul Lee who owns Lee's Kitchen, a restaurant in Tualatin. I asked him to help me find an individual in the Orient. We decided to make the trip together and were gone for two weeks. Paul was a delightful traveling companion. Not only did he speak several languages, but he was also a master in self-defense. It was quite comforting knowing I was traveling not only with an excellent interpreter, but a personal bodyguard as well.

We first went to Tokyo, then to Hong Kong, Bangkok, Macao and back to Hong Kong where we were finally able to find the person an attorney wanted to contact.

We did a great deal of shopping while we were in Hong Kong, and we stayed at a beautiful hotel with a huge cherry tree with artificial blossoms in the lobby. The tree was on an island in the middle of a pool of blue water. The tree measured about fifteen feet high, about thirty feet in circumference and boasted tens of thousands of artificial cherry blossoms. A wooden bridge led to an area under the tree where there was a grand piano. At night the guests would be entertained by lovely piano music, and after dinner we often found ourselves sitting in this serene setting, listening to the music and admiring the beautiful tree.

Paul Lee—my traveling companion in the Orient.
He is an excellent friend, interpreter and bodyguard. (1982)

We loved Thailand—it is very appropriately named the "Land of Smiles." Everyone seemed cheerful and happy. We stayed at a very nice hotel for several days and each day we would have a fabulous breakfast. We always sat at the same table in the restaurant and were served by the same delightful and attractive Thai waitress. She spoke English and seemed to enjoy our company. She shared with us that she earned about fifty American dollars a month and her tips were divided with the restaurant's owners. One morning she invited us to join her and her boyfriend for dinner at her parent's home. We thanked her, but gracefully declined her kind invitation.

After staying at the hotel for several days it was time to leave for Macao. When we finished our breakfast I asked our waitress if we could shake hands because we were leaving for the airport in a few minutes. She immediately extended her hand and when she withdrew it she found an American twenty-dollar bill in the palm of her hand. Paul also shook her hand and he also gave her a twenty. We had left moderate tips on the table each day that she could split with the restaurant owner. This young lady was absolutely overwhelmed to think that we had tipped her nearly a month's wage. She was so appreciative that she followed us out to the sidewalk asking if we would ever return to Thailand. We told her that this was a possibility after which she gave us her name and address with instructions on how to get in touch with her.

Before we left Bangkok we went into a large department store bought some jewelry, but not before haggling for quite some time about the price. This was expected. Imagine going in Macy's Department Store and saying, "Look, I will give you $100 for that $200 watch in the case."

During our Bangkok stay we took in a lot of the nightlife. We went to a huge disco where the dance floor covered almost an entire city block and the music never stopped. Everyone, and there must have been hundreds of couples dancing, was searched for weapons before they were allowed to enter. We were told this search was really more of a precaution than anything else; generally speaking the Thai people are well disciplined. Around seven o'clock one morning we were having breakfast, and the band was still playing and couples were still dancing.

In our search for the missing person we called on an official of the police known as an inspector. Paul talked with an inspector who was quite small in stature and then introduced him to me. The inspector looked at me and made a statement with a smile. Paul then turned to me and said the inspector was pleased to meet me and then commented that I was twice as big as he was. I told Paul to tell him that I might be twice his size, but that he was twice as smart. Paul interpreted this to the inspector after which he smiled broadly and cordially assisted us in our search.

There are a lot of elephants in Thailand. It is said there was a war in Thailand where 10,000 elephants were involved.

There were fresh orchids in our hotel room every day and from our window we could see barges being towed up river. Everywhere we went we met happy people. It is said that Thai people are born happy. I became acquainted with the hotel detective and for about a year after we left Thailand I continued to correspond with him. I don't know what happened, but his letters stopped and my letters were returned.

Paul and I visited many temples and the number of shaven monks surprised me. We visited the giant gold Buddha in one of the temples. Tourists could buy small paper pieces of gold to place on the giant Buddha for good luck.

We stopped in a restaurant for lunch, and Paul asked the attractive waitress for a lunch recommendation. Her suggestion was to try the extra delicious fried snake. I had Paul question her why the "extra delicious snake." She answered that the snakes were wild—mountain grown—and these snakes had a lot better taste than the home grown variety raised for restaurants. The waitress further shared that she came from the mountain area and that snake was only served on special occasions. This former farm girl also said they did not eat as much snake as they would have liked because the rich people in the village paid a lot of money for them. Even with all her instruction, we just couldn't bring ourselves to order the "organic" snake. However, if eating snake was in any way responsible for the exceptional beauty of our waitress, I would recommend fried snake to all young ladies.

We left Thailand, flew back to Hong Kong, and then took a fast hydroplane to the small island of Macao—probably the biggest gambling spot in the world. I was told not to talk to police officials, but I did, and found them to be very friendly and helpful. In this country we like our police force, but for some reason many Orientals fear and distrust the police and tend to shy away from them.

We left Macao and flew back to Hong Kong where Paul had a brother who owned a company that built foundations for skyscrapers. He had about 200 employees.

His brother entertained us in a lavish fashion and took us to many of Hong Kong's most famous restaurants. At one restaurant, the waiter brought large live shrimp to the table. A small heating device sat at the table and heated oil in a pan. The idea was to take one of the live shrimp, place it in the boiling oil for a few moments and then "bon appetite." Although I felt somewhat uncomfortable placing the shrimp in the hot oil with its big eyes staring at me, I got over it and found them to be absolutely delicious. You can't get any shrimp fresher than that.

A gentleman who was employed by Paul's brother volunteered to act as our tour guide while we were in Hong Kong. One night four of us went to a lively nightclub with an absolutely striking décor. The place was filled with many white statues, a beautiful indoor waterfall with a pond and an orchestra. Not only was the establishment beautiful, but it employed fifty gorgeous young Oriental ladies dressed in white silk gowns, and wearing an orchid, to sit at customers' tables and talk. The girls were paid for the time they spent with each customer. We were told there were gentlemen from a particular country that would spend as much as $5,000 an evening to talk to one of the girls. We were amused that our guide, Joe, said the only time he visited these clubs was when he had oversea guests or customers who wanted to see the town. However, this turned out to be not quite true. A young beautiful girl came to our table, looked at Joe and immediately said, "Joe, where have you been keeping yourself." Joe was quite embarrassed, particularly when she sat in his lap. I guess that's what you call "blowing your cover."

We also went to the horse races in Hong Kong. The track is the largest money track in the world as they take in the betting equivalent of about one million in American money for each race on a twelve-race card. Paul's brother had a box at the racetrack and when you were seated in the box you could hardly see the end of the line of people from each side—there were simply thousands placing bets.

We finally found the party we were looking for working in a Hong Kong bank. Our mission accomplished, we returned home.

The only problem we had on the entire trip was after we landed in Seattle. We arrived about noon and were to leave for Portland at five o'clock. When I learned that there were seats available on a 1:30 p.m. flight, I exchanged tickets and called the people who were to meet us about the change in our schedule. Unfortunately, we fell asleep while waiting for our 1:30 p.m. flight and didn't wake up until 2:30 p.m. (We were catching up on our sleep after a very busy time in the Orient.) Because we missed our flight, I had to exchange our tickets back to our original schedule. The airline ticket agent probably wondered why we couldn't make up our minds. More embarrassing was the fact that our greeters in Portland had rented a limousine to pick us up.

I continued operating the farm along with performing other additional incidental jobs. For example, I agreed to be the campaign manager for an individual running for county office. This may seem like a big title, but duties actually just involved making signs and placing them around the county.

At this time, I must bring "Kippie" into this story. Kippie was our German shepherd who lived with us on the farm. She was a great companion and we were lucky to have her with us for seventeen years. One morning I loaded my pickup with signs supporting my candidate, intending to place them at strategic intersections where the voting public could see them. I debated whether I should take Kippie with me, and finally decided she would be good company. She enjoyed riding with me and was always eager to get into the pickup. As it turned out, I was very fortunate that I decided to take her along.

Just as I was placing a campaign sign at an intersection in a rather remote area, a car came along with five young fellows inside. I did not pay any attention to them

Kippie and the apple orchard in full bloom. (1985)

until they honked and all gave me "the finger." I was still working on the sign when I noticed their car had stopped and was backing towards me. When I saw this, I walked over to my pickup. The five men got out of their truck and when they were about twenty feet away I opened the door of my pickup and grabbed Kippie by the leash. She immediately sensed the danger and began growling and jerking on her leash. She was aware that these rowdies were looking for trouble and were more or less out of control. It was obvious they had been drinking, but not to the extent that they didn't recognize the danger of the police dog. When they were about ten feet from Kippie, she really went into a war dance with a lot of snarling and showing her white teeth. It was obvious that to get to me they had to get by my dog. It was at a standstill when I called out to quiet Kippie, but not before saying I hoped I could restrain her or she would probably tear their legs off. I told them that I would give them about thirty seconds to leave me alone, or I would turn the dog loose. They only hesitated a brief moment before they turned around and went back to their car. I tried to obtain their license number but the plate was covered with mud. When I got back into my pickup with Kippie, I thanked my lucky stars that I had decided to take her along on what turned out to be more than "a ride."

On another occasion I was in the kitchen of the farmhouse when I heard Kippie barking. Looking out the window I saw her barking at something in the tree. I thought she had perhaps treed a cat, but she continued barking so I went outside to see what was bothering her. I went over to the tree, and much to my amazement I saw a man dressed in just shorts up in the branches. He was a jogger and I was so surprised I asked him what in the devil he was doing up in that tree. He explained that he was jogging through the orchard when my "damn dog" treed him. I told him that he was lucky and pointed out that I didn't want anyone jogging through the orchard. Actually, I really didn't mind people jogging through the orchard but I was concerned if they stepped in a hole and broke a leg I would probably be involved in a lawsuit.

Another Kippie incident occurred one day as I was plowing a field. Kippie always joined me in the field and, at times, would follow the tractor. On this particular occasion, she took off and I didn't miss her until she began circling the tractor. She had something in her mouth and was trying to get my attention as much as I was trying to ignore her. Eventually, she stopped right in front of the tractor forcing me to come to a halt. Kippie looked at the ground and then at me, her tail wagging like crazy. I got down from the tractor and went to her side. It was quite obvious she had brought me a present, and as I got right up to her I could see her present was nothing less than a royal cut of a T-bone steak. I wondered where Kippie could have gotten such "a prize" since the entire field was fenced in. I then remembered she would go through a tile of the creek under a steel fence that led to a large apartment complex adjoining my farm. Obviously, she had gone through the tile up to the apartments and "found" herself a choice cut of meat. I gazed up at the apartments and saw a man standing on a deck next to a barbecue grill. He was looking at his barbecue and it was obvious he was missing something. There was no question he was looking for the steak Kippie had brought me. The man had apparently gone into his apartment to get something, and when he came back his steak was gone. I could not help but be amused as he looked everywhere for the missing piece of meat—underneath the barbecue, around it and finally up at the sky to see if some bird had swooped down and stolen his dinner. Later, I went over to his apartment to pay for the steak, but he wasn't home. I slipped a five dollar bill under his door.

One day, Kippie came to the farmhouse and barked to get my attention. I went outside and followed her to the street where a young man was lying on the sidewalk. He had been stabbed in the leg and there was a pool of blood on the roadway. He begged me not to call the police, but I told him he had to have medical attention after which the police would be called. I told the police I would like to hear how the young man eventually made out, but I was never contacted. I've always thought the entire episode resulted from a drug deal gone wrong, but I never found out anything definite.

While I was farming I would occasionally hire a young man to help with the work. I once hired the son of a friend of mine and it didn't turn out very well. Now, I don't recommend hiring friend's relatives. The problem was his father said his son was a tremendous worker and really wanted a job. Unfortunately, that didn't prove to be true. The young man did not have any interest in his work and I was wondering how I was going to get rid of him. Finally, I had a solution. I knew the father would be upset if I simply fired his son, so I questioned the young man in more detail when he said he did not know why he was working for only $7 an hour. He told me that his girlfriend told him that he could be making $150 an hour modeling. I told him I did not want him to come back to work the following day; that I was not going to spoil his chance of a lifetime of making $150 an hour. I told him to go for it and I would get someone else to replace him. Several weeks later I met his father who asked me why his son was not working for me. I innocently told him that his son had advised me what he could make more modeling, and I was not going to stand in his way from making that kind of money. Apparently, his son never got the job because his father raised his eyes skyward and said, "How could you believe such a story?" I didn't think he knew I was putting him on. He most likely thought I must be very stupid.

One of my friends, a Chinese restaurant owner, brought over his two young nephews from China to permanently reside in the United States. It was time to harvest the Love apple crop, so I hired them to help pick the apples. They could not speak English and had no apple picking experience, but I was able to communicate with them in sign language. I showed them how the apples were to be picked and placed in boxes. They were excellent workers. I noticed they would spend their lunch hour sitting in the farm pickup. They had never driven an automobile and they would just sit behind the wheel, turn it this way and that and pretend to drive. As a treat at the end of the day I permitted them to drive the pickup around in the field in low gear while I sat next to them with my hand on the brake. The pickup went around and around that field—first one and then the other taking a turn driving. It was quite a sight seeing one of them driving while the other ran behind the slow moving pickup yelling in Chinese that it was his turn to drive. Kippie, of course, joined in the fun by barking and following the runner behind the pickup. I wondered what the people driving on the street could possibly think was going on as they watched this strange sight of the pickup going around and around.

From the first day until they completed picking the apples, they learned enough about driving the pickup to be able to handle it well enough on their own. It was a pleasure to be able to give both of these fine young men their first job in America and their first driving lesson.

After about ten years in America, they own a Chinese restaurant, beautiful homes and drive late model cars. Their work ethic is something to talk about. The fathers started as dishwashers and then became cooks, their sons learned how to cook, the daughters worked as waitresses and the mothers as dishwashers. It's a nice story of a family working together and achieving success.

As the crops were growing through the summer, I had about ten sprinklers with a pump drawing water out of the spring creek. Kippie really enjoyed running through the sprinklers as did some of the area's smaller children when the weather turned hot.

It was necessary to cut the grass in the Love apple orchard about every two weeks. We used a mower with a five-foot cut pulled by a 1930 one-lung-popping John Deere tractor. It was a Model L and it ran like a John Deere and kept running like a John Deere throughout the spring and summer. One day the radiator sprang a leak. I called the John Deere dealer and asked one of his salesmen if they had a radiator for a Model L. The tractor was so old that he was not acquainted with the model. Finally, he said he would look for a radiator, after which I jokingly asked if the warranty was still good because, after all, the tractor was only about fifty years old. I believe he took me seriously and, ultimately, thought I was some kind of a nut.

This model was aptly named "popping" because it made that kind of sound when it was running. That sound was like a magnet to all of the neighborhood kids. One of our neighbors was a couple with five small children. One day I was mowing near their backyard and all the children were watching. They seemed so fascinated that I finally stopped and picked up one of the small boys and placed him on my lap. I let him steer the tractor while I held on to him with my foot on the brake. This really started something, for it wasn't but a moment and the other four children also wanted a ride. They all enjoyed the ride so much that their father, Steve Nistler, a wonderful man with a wonderful family, made a deal with me. The deal was that he would mow the orchard every week giving each of his children a ride, and I would have my grass cut. It worked out great for both of us. His children were thoroughly entertained and I could sleep under a tree as the eight acres of grass were cut.

Kippie lived to be seventeen. She was very ill when I took her to the vet to have her put to sleep. The day the vet lifted her from the back of my pickup to the clinic's gurney was one of the saddest ever for my brother and me. I was acquainted with the lady who worked for the government and originally purchased Kippie. After owning the dog for six months she was transferred to Guam and could not take her along. She wanted to find Kippie a good home and wouldn't let us take her until she came to the farm and inspected our home and the surroundings. I don't know where that lady is today, but I want her to know that Kippie had a wonderful life. I wrote her once about two months after we had gotten Kippie. I wrote the letter as if Kippie had written it. It read, "I am thinking of going to obedience school, but my family really does not feel I need to. My family really loves me and I really like it here on the farm. I get to roam around and I even jump into the creek when it gets hot. Thanks for finding me such a good home." I'll never forget Kippie and the wonderful moments of companionship we shared over the years.

Several years had gone by after I retired from the railroad and I found myself thinking about going back to work as an investigator. It was just about this time that I received an invitation for a Christmas lunch from two attorneys, Jim Pippin and Mark Bocci. When I worked for the railroad, these two attorneys were adversaries and I handled quite a number of cases with them. I liked and respected them as they were honest and straightforward in their approach to handling a case and always placed their client's interest ahead of their own. While we were having lunch, Jim Pippin asked me if I would consider working for them as an investigator. I told him that even though I would like to, that I could not because they were still handling a few cases against the railroad; the railroad had treated me well and I did not want to work against the company. Jim told me they had many other cases that did not involve the railroad, and asked if I would work on those. I had no problem with that and I accepted their offer.

I had worked for almost thirty years on the defense side of the coin and was very curious to see what the other side was like. Interestingly, I found that it was easier inves-

I investigated this car accident. The car wrapped around a telephone pole while traveling at a very high rate of speed. The imprint of the telephone pole can easily be seen in the center of the automobile.
(1985)

tigating cases for plaintiffs than for defendants. It was so much easier to talk to a witness about an injured person. Usually the conversation started out with the witness asking if "the poor old lady was getting over her injuries." Sympathy for the injured party is usually in the picture.

I recall a case where a small boy scooted out of the driveway on his bicycle and was hit by a car. A neighbor lady told me that there was nothing the driver of the car could do to avoid the accident because the boy popped out into the street. Six months later when I talked to her again, she changed her story and said the driver was going too fast.

This particular accident happened in my neighborhood and, after a little while, the neighbors wanted to put in a bicycle path. They wanted to know if the railroad had any old ties that they could use to brace the dirt shoulders along the path. I went to a good friend of mine, Chief District

Engineer Haacke, and another friend, Vice-President Howard Burnett, and it worked out that we could have several truckloads of ties from an old feeder line in Hood River. Early one Saturday morning the neighbors rented a truck, loaded the ties and brought them to the designated places where the ties were to be placed. I will always remember that day because after working about fourteen hours I went to an opera in Portland that lasted four hours. As it turned out, I was so tired that I slept through the entire opera. After the bicycle path was built the kids hardly ever used it because they liked the paved road much better. Had I known this, I would have worked fewer hours on the bicycle path and enjoyed the opera more.

I have enjoyed a wonderful relationship with the Pippin & Bocci law firm for almost twenty years. The firm consists of only the two lawyers (brothers-in-law) and they do not want to expand. They gave me a free hand in my investigative work and eventually they treated me as family, not as an employee. I guess that I worked nearly 300 cases for them over the years. Peg and Beth worked in the office and did a great job of keeping everyone in line. I enjoyed an open telephone line with them—day or night—and had authorization to incur any bills that in my judgment were necessary to complete the work.

I investigated a case for the Pippin & Bocci firm that involved a baby injured in an auto accident. There was a significant question about the seat belt not holding her securely at the time of the accident. I contacted various witnesses, but I was mainly interested in speaking with the person who took the baby out of the car following the accident. The baby was removed because of the fear of fire. I contacted a witness who was listed on the police report and he informed me he had removed the baby uninjured from her seat after the accident. He indicated the baby was facing the front of the car at the time he removed the seat. This was an error because the baby should have been placed in its seat facing the back of the seat or the rear of the car. This placed the blame on the mother for improperly seating her baby in the car. I continued the investigation because the mother insisted she had correctly placed the baby in the car seat. Several weeks later I contacted another witness who quite surprisingly told me that he had removed the baby from the car and that the baby was facing toward the rear of the car. Here I had two versions of who removed the baby from the car. I then returned to the first witness and told him that I was really puzzled as to who removed the baby from the car. I told him that another witness, now out-of-state, definitely stated he had removed the baby. I then suggested that perhaps he had made an error as to who removed the baby from the car. I pointed out there was another witness who recalled the out-of-state witness removing the baby and, in fact, she had taken the seat from him and placed it on the ground. The witness then said he undoubtedly was mistaken about removing the baby because there was so much confusion going around and he was afraid the car might catch on fire with all the spilled gasoline. I took a supplemental statement contradicting what he originally told me. Shortly thereafter the case settled.

At Mark Bocci's request I investigated an accident at the Reno airport. I arrived on a Sunday afternoon at three o'clock. A little later I was at a poker table with a quarter limit. I am not a heavy gambler but I like to play a little poker on a rare occasion and sometimes bet on the greyhounds. I sat down at a poker table since I had time to kill. I played till midnight, and was about $850 ahead. I thought I would run the money up to an even $1,000 and then call it quits but, alas, when I finally stopped at two o'clock I was about $200 behind in my own money. This was the first trip I ever made to Reno, and I learned that the men playing in the game were no dummies. I told Mark when I finished the case that he should pay me an additional $200 fee to cover my poker loss. I told him that had he not sent me there I would not have been playing poker. Surprisingly, he did not see it my way.

When my son was in high school, his school (Sunset High) was playing Gresham High. A neighbor, Judd Killpack, who also had a son at Sunset, and I went to the game together. After the game was over, we decided to go to the nearby dog track to bet on a few races. We arrived at one of the late races and bought a racing program. We sat down and gave it a good going over — calculating how the dog came out of the box, whether it liked to run inside or outside and how strong it finished. I decided I would put about $10 on the No. 3 dog to win. He was a three-to-one favorite. I opened my wallet on my way to the window to purchase the ticket and found that I had only taken a $5 bill to the football game with me. I was quite irritated at myself. When I was at the ticket window instead of calling out $5 to win on No. 3, I said $5 on No. 5. They say that once you make a mistake in buying a ticket to never exchange it so I found myself stuck with the wrong dog. I took my No. 5 ticket to where my neighbor was standing and he asked me what dog I bet. I looked up on the odds board and it read that the No. 5 dog was thirty-to-one. I then looked at the program where it showed that No. 5 was a slow breaker; that he liked to run from the outside (he had an inside box), he was a poor finisher and this was a long race. I didn't want to own up to my neighbor about my stupid mistake so I did not answer him. The race ran and No. 5 won defying all the expert information. For my $5 bet on its nose to win, I received $150. After the race my neighbor asked, "Really, who did you bet on?" as he threw his losing ticket on the floor. I told him I bet on the five dog—the winner. He then wanted to see my ticket because he did not believe me. After looking at the ticket with a puzzled expression he asked, "How in the world did you know?" I said, "Judd, when you are out here betting hard-earned money, you've got to know what you're doing." He simply shook his head but my answer seemed to satisfy him. I guess he just couldn't argue with success. Later, I heard from other neighbors how fantastic I was at picking out thirty-to-one longshots. Some of them suggested we go to the races but, of course, I was always too busy to prove my newfound skill at the races.

Actually, my history with greyhounds goes back a long way. I was first introduced to greyhounds and greyhound racing in the 1930s as a teenager when George Carroll, a greyhound owner, asked me to be his trainer during the summer when his dogs ran in Portland. In those days, all the greyhounds kenneled in rented barns in the Beaverton area and Mr. Carroll, now deceased, walked his dogs by our farm quite often. He noticed how hard I worked in the fields, and later he asked me to be his trainer because he felt that if I worked as hard for him as I did on the farm, I would do a good job for him. I don't believe my father was particularly fond of the idea, but he relented as I finished all my farm chores in the afternoon so that I could work with the dogs in the morning and go to the track with them in the evening. I really liked being a trainer and was grateful to have such a good paying summer job—five dollars a week.

Back then, the races took place on a track where Multnomah Athletic Club and Civic Stadium are today. In those days, the dogs didn't break from boxes, but from leather harnesses. During its early history, the races attracted huge crowds. It was not uncommon for a derby race to draw 30,000 people. You had to walk one-half mile from the track to find a place to park. The results of the previous night's dog races were discussed around many a table the next day.

Being so young, I felt fortunate to have the opportunity to train some great winners.

We had a class dog by the name of "My Profit." He liked the name "Tom" but would not answer to "Tommy." He was a quiet dog with a champion's air about him. You could just tell he was something special. He had a fantastic win record in my first season of training and qualified for the season-ending derby. I gave Tom his last instructions a few hours prior to our leaving for Multnomah Stadium for the race. I told him, "Tom, they have brought the best dogs in the country to this race just to smoke you over. What *we* have to do is come out of the harness like a rocket, hug the rail, run like the wind and when we hit the homestretch really open it up." Tom looked up at me as if to say he understood my instructions but wondered about the "*we*" part. I gave him a big hug, loaded him into the trailer and headed for the track.

The race started, and Tom came out of his harness like he had been shot out of a cannon. He ran superbly (just a little ahead of the other dogs) and when he reached the homestretch, all the other dogs saw of him was his dust all the way to the finish line. He won "going away"—a wonderful victory. Mr. Carroll won a great deal of money and I earned a $100 trainer's bonus—a huge amount of money for a high school boy during the Depression.

Although there was quite a fanfare after Tom won the race, including a presentation of flowers, a trophy and a live band playing marching songs, he seemed completely indifferent and bored by all the attention. He didn't perk up until later at the kennel when George gave him a beautiful steak and I gave him several gingersnap cookies I had purchased earlier that day.

Tom repeated his winning ways, including the derby the following year, and was only one of three dogs in seventy years of racing in Portland to win more than one derby race.

Tom came from an outstanding litter of pups. His little sister, "Little Profit" (nicknamed Penny), ran third in the derby and his big brother, "Big Profit" (nicknamed Moose), ran fourth. All of these dogs had distinct personalities. Penny was a very friendly little dog who could really run. Moose could also run, but he was lazy. Let's just say his nickname fit him perfectly. He was always banging into things and I always had difficulty getting him into his kennel.

I was amazed to discover that the dogs remembered me when they returned to Portland from winter racing in Florida. They barked excitedly and ran over to greet me in their pen.

They never had such races in Portland, but old-timers in the racing business told me that in the early days of racing monkeys were strapped on the greyhounds' backs as jockeys. They said that it was quite a thing to watch, but that the practice was stopped when too many of the monkeys were injured.

The greyhounds also ran hurdle races. The dogs ran around the track and jumped hurdles as they went. We had quite a hurdler named "Chain Gang." He was a great jumper and seemed to just float over the hurdles.

I occasionally go to the dog track now and find that it brings back a lot of pleasant memories of my early days. I am glad to see adoption programs have been implemented to find homes for the old retired racers. They do make great pets. I should know.

I investigated an airplane accident in which five men, including the pilot of the plane, were killed when the plane crashed into the Kautz Glacier on Mt. Rainier. The single engine Cessna 210 smashed nose first at about the 12,500' level of the 14,000' high mountain. One of the victims was a young man, Mike Currin, from Eastern Oregon. He was an outstanding rodeo performer in college and had a great future in rodeos according to the people I talked to in the industry.

I called on the parents of this young man and found them to be good down-to-earth, hard-working ranchers. They were easy to talk with in spite of their grief over their son's death. I learned that they had three sons in the rodeo near Portland where they were performing. All three sons had made arrangements to fly on the ill-fated plane to Ponoka, Canada, to perform in that city. One of them called their parents and told them they were leaving in a few minutes for Ponoka, but two of the brothers switched planes at the very last moment. The parents didn't know this when they received initial word that the plane had crashed. They just

assumed that all three sons had been lost. As terrible as it
was losing one son, they were overjoyed later when they
found out two of the sons had taken another flight.

My investigation in the case included gathering information about the young man who lost his life. He had a
tremendous potential—not only as a rodeo performer, but
also as an individual. The other young men in the plane
were also outstanding performers with a bright future.

Jim Pippin asked me to investigate a serious intersection accident in Portland. A lady driving a Buick entered an
intersection when another car slammed into her. She suffered
serious injuries, but the four occupants of the other car were
not injured. The lady stated the other vehicle was being driven
at a high rate of speed in a residential area. The four occupants in the other car stated this was not true—that the driver
of the Buick was "going to a fire." Whose version would a
jury accept? The count was four to one against our client, the
driver of the Buick.

I discussed the case with Jim Pippin and told him that I
had contacted everyone connected with the accident but I was
unable to find an independent witness who saw the accident.
Jim had a feeling someone witnessed the accident and directed me to go back out and try again. I went to each house
for two or three blocks from where the accident happened to
see if I could find an eyewitness. I was trying to find someone who might have been working in their yard or looking
out their window when the cars went by. I even contacted the
Mayor of Portland, Frank Ivancie, who resided on a street
leading to the intersection. He was very nice and went so far
as to check his date book. He told me that he could not have
been a witness because he had been in Japan that day.

Jim kept insisting there had to be a witness, and encouraged me to keep looking. I then went to the police officer
who investigated the accident. I asked him if he would be so
kind as to look at his notes on the accident for possible names.
After checking his notes, he came up with a name but his

notes also reflected that this witness had not seen the accident. I contacted this individual and BINGO. I hit the jackpot. He was a bright young college student. He said he had been coming from the opposite direction of the car approaching the Buick, and when he saw the other car a block away it was coming at him at a tremendously fast speed. He said that just before the impact, he pulled over to the side of the street, stopped and placed his hands over his eyes because he did not want to see the impact. I questioned him why he had not furnished this information to the police. He told me the policeman asked him if he "saw" the impact. Because his hands were over his eyes, he answered negatively.

This was only one example where one of Jim's "hunches" proved correct. The earlier four-to-one count against our Buick driver turned out to be one big zero for the opposition.

This young fellow was a very cooperative witness.
I asked him to show me where the injured man was when he first
saw him. I only wanted him to stand and point, but when I was
walking away to take the picture he decided to really show me.
I was quite surprised when I turned around to take the picture
and he was there on the sidewalk. (1987)

When not working for Pippin & Bocci I had all the work I could handle with other attorneys, but it was always understood that Pippin & Bocci came first. At times I worked for the State of Oregon, several insurance companies and numerous other attorneys. I received a number of calls to work on divorce cases, but I stayed completely away from those. When working for the wife, the husband is angry with you. When working for the husband, the wife is angry with you. It is a one-way street and a lose/lose situation as far as feelings are concerned.

A lady called me one day and said she needed an investigator. I asked her who her attorney was and she said she hadn't retained one. I told her that I only worked for attorneys, and she asked me if her money wasn't just as good as an attorney's. I was amused by her comeback and asked her to describe her problem. She wanted me to look for "Cicero." I asked her who Cicero was. She told me it was her mischievous poodle, who had been missing for about a month. I suggested rather than spending a lot of money on an investigator to find Cicero, it might be better to buy another poodle. She said, "No. I have money and even if you looked for and didn't find Cicero, I would feel much better to know that I made the effort—so would Cicero." She was determined to retain an investigator to look for her poodle so I referred her to an honest investigator, Michelle Olson, who told me later that she searched for Cicero around the neighborhood and then presented her with a modest bill. The client was pleased and gave her a gift certificate in addition to the fee. An unscrupulous investigator could have had a field day with this case. I can just imagine a corrupt investigator advising her daily (at $50 an hour) how close he was to finding Cicero. In fact, the investigator could have said he had a lead that someone took Cicero to Las Vegas where further investigation should be done. On the other hand, perhaps the more money she spent to find Cicero, the better she felt. Obviously, this lady was very fond of Cicero, and she should be complimented for being that concerned about her pet.

A man who was a friend of a friend of mine told me he had a problem. His son had parked his pickup at a public building. When he returned to it he discovered that someone had backed into his pickup and caused damage. He wanted to retain me to investigate to find the hit-and-run driver. After he told me the damage was not quite $100, I said it would probably be better to pay that amount to have the car repaired than to pay a lot more money to retain an investigator who might or might not find the culprit. The man replied, "No. My son worked hard to buy the pickup." He wanted me to show his son that whoever did the damage had to pay for it regardless of the cost for investigating the matter. In view of this, I took the assignment and eventually found the hit-and-run driver who denied that he had a part in the accident. I then matched the two cars as to damage points, and the results confirmed my findings. The hit-and-run driver stated that he had not been driving the car at the time. I told him to stop making excuses—that he had a choice—either pay for the damages or his name would be turned in for hit-and-run. I also told him to add $50 for my investigation fee—which I gave to the boy who had worked all summer to pay for the pickup. The following day the young man handed over a cashier's check for the full amount. I had to smile when I was interviewing a young lad of high school age in this case. I introduced myself as an investigator at which time his eyes opened wide and he said, "You mean like Barnaby Jones?"

I worked an extremely sad and serious case involving two four-year-old boys who had been playing in the laundry room of an apartment complex. Someone had stored a five-gallon can of gas in the laundry room, and one of the boys tipped over the gas can, and the contents ran on the floor to a clothes dryer that was operating. The sparks set off the gas and the explosion killed one of the boys outright, and seriously injured the other youngster. It was a horrible accident as the boy who lived had burns over eighty percent of his body. He lived for about six months and then died after many operations. I never could figure out why the boy had to suffer for six months only to finally die. I mention this case to reveal that I had a lot of sad cases along with those that had happier endings.

In nearly fifty years as an investigator did I ever work on a case that involved me personally? Yes, I did. On September 7, 1996, I opened my mail and found a letter containing a speeding ticket based on photo radar. The ticket indicated that the speed limit on Center Street was twenty-five miles per hour and I was traveling thirty-five miles per hour when the photo machine got me. My impression was that the speed limit on Center Street for years had been thirty-five miles per hour. This was confirmed by a police officer a number of years ago when he asked permission to park in my driveway to catch drivers for failing to obey a stop sign at the intersection. There were no signs posted when 800 speeding tickets were issued from September 7th into November. About this time, my breakfast members (comprised of mostly Beaverton businessmen) jokingly pounced on me asking, "How I was going to get out of this one." In fact, one morning when I arrived for breakfast, I saw they had posted signs on the restaurant's doors and tables reading: "Stop Criminal Injustice—Help Free Louie—Donation Headquarters", "Free Louie—He Didn't Mean to Do It," and "Don't Let Louie Go to the Slammer."

I appeared in Municipal Court and pleaded "Not guilty," however, there were about sixty-five other drivers who paid their fines. My trial came up several weeks later. Pippin and Bocci volunteered to appear in court for me if I so desired. I told them I would try this one myself and, if I failed,

STOP CRIMINAL INJUSTICE
HELP FREE LOUIE
DONATION HEADQUARTERS

DON'T LET LOUIE GO TO THE SLAMMER

"FREE LOUIE"

HE DIDN'T MEAN

TO DO IT!

I would bring them in as the battleships at the final appeal. In the latter part of November, I again went to court and brought out the following facts:

> (1) Speed signs were placed on the street in the latter part of October—after 800 tickets were issued;

> (2) I presented a certified letter dated October 11th from the City of Beaverton to the State of Oregon requesting the speed be rescinded from the present 35 mph to 25 mph. This was after 800 tickets had been issued for going 35 mph;

> (3) I presented an additional certified letter from the State of Oregon, which I had obtained at the State Capital in Salem. This letter, dated the latter part of October after 800 tickets were issued, stated the City of Beaverton had their permission to reduce the speed on Center Street from 35 mph to 25 mph;

> (4) I introduced a map showing the portion of the street were I was ticketed was in the county and not in the city which indicated the city had no jurisdiction over this area;

(5) I had information from the county showing the speed to be 35 mph; and

(6) I told the court that in view of the fact the police officer who testified had ticketed forty-five drivers in one four-hour session something was drastically wrong. I believed the police should have taken immediate action when that many tickets were issued in a four-hour period. I also pointed out that if the situation was truly so dangerous that 800 tickets had been issued, then speed signs should have been immediately placed there and not three months after the "gold vein" ran out.

The judge, who I did not recognize until after my case was heard, was at one time a county prosecutor who called me on a case involving a float plane that struck and killed two persons in a canoe when it was skimming over the water. I had investigated the case and was subpoenaed to testify against the pilot.

After the judge ruled I was not guilty, I went up to him, and he said he was wondering where he had seen me before the trial.

A businessman, a city representative and I were talking after the trial and the businessman pointed out that if I was not guilty then how about the 800 others who had received tickets? The representative spoke up and said, "You do not expect us to pay them back around $80,000?" My friend replied, "Well, if Lou is not guilty then why should the others be guilty?"

Even though most of the drivers pleaded guilty, the City of Beaverton announced in the paper within a day or two after my court appearance that they were going to put on their white hats and for Christmas would refund the money to the holders of all the speeding tickets.

Elaine Murphy, a sharp television reporter, interviewed me on TV and I commented on the tickets.

The next day at the breakfast meeting I was told justice was served. I was especially pleased when an elderly lady called and thanked me for "fighting City Hall." She had been coming home from church one day and had received a ticket. She told me she was looking forward to receiving her refund, and wanted to bake me some cookies as a "Thank You." She was a good baker.

You know, I can't begin to count the number of police officers I have contacted in the course of conducting my investigations and I never found one I disliked. They typically do an excellent job of making out reliable and detailed accident reports, including sketches, etc. and furnishing information for all involved parties. I always made it a personal policy not to inconvenience them any more than was absolutely necessary. If I had to discuss an accident with a deputy sheriff, city policeman, state trooper or other law enforcement officer who went to work at midnight, I would contact them at the beginning (midnight) of their shift rather than at the end (8:00 A.M.). I took into consideration that the officer had worked the entire night, had reports to make and was anxious to get home to enjoy what other people do in their spare time. Many of them were surprised that I would contact them at midnight and asked me why.

I worked a number of sad criminal and civil cases for different attorneys. One case involved a young mother who allegedly killed her baby. I won't go into the details of the case, but after my investigation, I was not convinced that she killed her baby. I talked to her alone in a law library and pointing out that I thought she was protecting someone else who had actually smothered her baby. I strongly suggested she give this matter a great deal of thought because if it was true that someone else had committed murder, then that person would go free and she would be incarcerated. I dropped my voice, and for about five minutes there was complete silence after which she finally shook her head and said that she was the guilty party. She pleaded guilty and the facts of my investigation were revealed to the judge who sentenced her. All I can say is that love creates strong bonds.

I worked a case in Spokane for Richard Kuhling, an outstanding attorney, where a mentally unbalanced young man shot and killed an individual and then killed himself. A relative sued the state and other parties alleging that the young man should not have been released from a state institution. The crime occurred in a small farm community in a rather remote mountain area and, like a lot of little towns, there was excessive use of drugs—even by the younger set. I arrived in town in the morning and proceeded to investigate the matter, particularly seeking facts about the young man involved. The following morning I had breakfast with the district attorney who told me that the entire town was aware that I was an investigator. The news spread that there was a big time drug investigator from the coast working in their town. I paid little attention to this since I had nothing to do with drugs, other than discovering facts about the possibility of drugs being involved in the shooting. I gave this more attention later when I realized how serious the talk was about a drug investigator being in town. Late on the second day, I went into a grocery store to purchase some articles. When I came out of the store it was dusk and as I stepped through the door someone took a flash picture of me, and a longhaired fellow ran to a pickup and took off in a hurry. There was no license plate on the pickup. Apparently, someone wanted me to know they knew I was in the area and checking on drugs. My investigation revealed that one group that had graduated from high school had serious drug problems. In later life, two members of the group died of drug overdoses, three were in drug rehabilitation centers and several committed suicide.

I entered a tavern one night to locate a witness and the patrons all moved to separate tables. It reminded me of a western movie when the gunfighter walked into a saloon. I worked in that town for about a week and was surprised to find out that Angel Dust was one of the leading drugs used in the town, although there was considerable marijuana grown in the mountain area. I turned my large investigation file over to the three defendants after which the case was settled.

Although I mainly concentrated on cases with the Pippin & Bocci law firm, I would occasionally work a case for an outside attorney during slack time. An out-of-state attorney called advising he represented a client whose fifteen-year-old daughter had run away from home. They suspected she was somewhere in the Portland area. He said a search had already been made, but she could not be found. I told him to send me her photograph and I would see what I could do to locate her. After spending a number of nights on the streets and questioning all kinds of people in various establishments, I thought I had located her working in a strip joint. At least I was told that a dancer at the joint looked a great deal like her. It turned out the stripper was not who I was looking for—although there was an amazing resemblance—and it was back to the drawing board.

I finally found her one evening on the street in a not-so-good part of town. She was actually very happy that I had located her, especially after I told her that her parents were deeply concerned about her and they loved her very much. I also mentioned that her parents were paying me a good sum of money to find her. She wanted to go home, so I took her to dinner and then to a hotel where I rented her a room for the night. I told her I would pick her up in the morning, put her on a bus home, and have her parents meet the bus. She was very excited and it was obvious she had her stomach full about running away.

That evening I called the attorney and told him to have her folks meet the bus in the morning. The attorney asked me if I thought it was necessary that I accompany her on the bus, or should her parents drive to Portland to pick her up. I said this was not necessary as she had enough of being away, and was really ready to go home. The next morning I picked her up at her hotel, fed her a good breakfast and took her to the bus station. Later that day I received word from the attorney that the family had reunited and were very happy. Several weeks later I received a phone call from the girl's father who told me everything was working out perfectly and that he wanted to thank me for finding his daughter. I told him that it was not such a big deal—that she would have probably gone back home by herself had I not found her. He said this was true, but she needed a push. Also, being without funds and encouragement someone else might have picked up on her, and that could have changed her life. He then said if I was ever in their city to give him a call, and he would take me to a nice dinner. I never visited their city, but my work on the case gave me more satisfaction on a personal level than monetary rewards. Fortunately, this girl had parents who cared. Unfortunately, there are many similar cases where the parents do not care, contributing to the sad state of affairs in our society.

On another case I was asked to find a bartender with a spotty employment record. I went to his last place of known employment. It turned out to be a nightclub in produce row that catered to Lesbians. I entered the establishment and was surprised to see female couples dancing to music from a jukebox. I went up to the female bartender and asked her if she had any information concerning the whereabouts of the bartender I was trying to find. She kindly told me that the establishment had been taken over by a new owner, and the bartender was working a certain club downtown. I thanked her and worked myself toward the door through about twenty couples who were dancing. When I opened the door, I noticed a somewhat attractive lady smiling at me on my right by the door, and a tough looking lady on my left also near the door. I was smiling at both of them as I was passing through the doorway, when the lady on the left stuck her foot out and deliberately tripped me. I fell to my knees on the cement sidewalk. As I was getting up with pain in my knees, I was furious and my first thought was to strike out with a blow. However, I controlled myself and said of all things, "Pardon me," and walked out to my car. As I was sitting in my car filled with anger, the attractive lady came to me and apologized for her friend's behavior. I thanked her for seeking me out and, after driving a few blocks, I cooled down and was thankful I handled the situation the way I did. If I had entered into an altercation with her I don't know what the final outcome would have been. But, in any event, I would have been the loser. I certainly did not need newspaper publicity or any other kind that I struck a woman in a fight.

On one case I was instructed to find a witness involved in a criminal case. She was a nude dancer and I first went to her father who told me he did not know her whereabouts but suggested she might be in jail. I checked various women's prisons in the area but had no luck. Some of her friends said she was undoubtedly in the state and could not understand why she could not be located. I searched and searched, keeping in mind what the "chief" told me when I first started to investigate cases for the railroad—"Don't come back until the witness is found, or you know where they are buried." I spent many days searching and finally I came to the conclusion that she had to be in jail—even though I was advised a month previous by several penal institutions that she was not in their jail. On my second check I discovered that she was an inmate and that the person I checked with a month before had made a mistake.

I was asked to locate a witness who was a nude dancer two years earlier when a policeman was killed. This was a real tough assignment. I usually make my first approach by saying, "Look, I am not in any way connected with the police, and I am not a bill collector or a process server." These people are friendly, but they are guarded in giving out information as to the whereabouts of their co-workers. They simply do not want to get involved. I first went to an employment agency that receives a fee for placing dancers at various establishments. Even with this source of information it is difficult to locate the witness because they usually use a stage name. In addition, I was told by an agency that there are about 600 of these girls working in the Portland area. Another problem—for the most part, they are not steady performers. Many of them quit for other jobs, others return to school making it more difficult to locate them.

In this particular case, I found the witness working as a secretary in the mid-west. After talking with her she agreed to come to Portland and testify in the civil case in behalf of the police officer's dependents. After we brought her to Portland the case was settled before trial.

When taking statements I have made it a point to conclude the statement by asking how they can be located should they move to another address or another location. I ask them to identify someone who would know their whereabouts if they move from the area and make a note of their answer for possible future use. Many of the cases where I was assigned to locate a witness could have been avoided had this been done at the time of the initial contact.

When I started working for the Pippin & Bocci law firm, they didn't have enough investigative work to keep me busy on a steady basis. This changed however, as more cases came into the firm, and I worked almost exclusively for Jim and Mark. In the meantime, they were kind enough to recommend me to other attorneys. One of the attorneys they referred me to was Michael Shinn.

Michael represented the estate of a woman who had been murdered. Because of his victory in the civil trial, the prosecuting attorney was able to successfully try the husband for murder five years after the murder. The criminal trial resulted in a life sentence for the husband. This interesting criminal case was written up in the book "Dead By Sunset" by the well known author, Ann Rule. Michael is also associated with the renowned attorney, Jerry Spence, from Wyoming.

Michael was a true athlete and one of the best quarterbacks Willamette University ever had. Michael Shinn is a friend of my son, Ron, and together they played for the Portland Pigs, a rugby team. The player roster of this team was quite unique in that it consisted of a number of attorneys, businessmen and several physicians. It was not uncommon for the physicians use their professional skills on injured players during the games.

I had never been to a rugby game until my son invited me to watch a game at Delta Park in Portland. Now football is rough but, if you want to see an extremely rough game, watch a rugby match. It, quite simply, is mayhem. The players do not wear protective pads or helmets. They play in shorts and T-shirts. In football, hitting the kicker is a serious penalty, in rugby, the kicker is "fair game" and the idea is to tackle him when he is in the process of kicking the ball. It is also permissible for teammates to carry the player with the ball forward when trying to score. Of course, the *fun* starts when the opposing team not only tries to prevent the "flying wedge" from scoring, but also does everything it can to take the ball away from the carrier.

The game I attended was played on a rainy day and the field was nothing but one big mud hole. During the game, a fight broke out and one of the Canadian players sustained damage to his teeth. The "Pig" who threw the punch took the Canadian to his personal dentist after the game. It was nice to see how friendly the players were to each other *after* the game.

I was introduced to the Canadian coach, who turned out to be an Englishman. After he was told that this was the first rugby game I had ever seen, he asked me how I liked it. I remarked that it certainly was spirited and said that I would be available to play if he ever came up short a player. You know, I think he took me seriously because he said, "Well, let's leave it this way—I'll call you. Don't you call me."

Jim Gidley, an excellent trial attorney for whom I had worked in the past, was a football player in college and also played for the Portland Pigs. What a contrast! Instead of seeing him impeccably dressed in a suit pleading his case to a jury, he was covered from head to toe in a suit of mud. Rumor had it that during rugby season it was not uncommon for him to arrive in his office on Monday morning after a rugby weekend courting a black eye or two.

Harvey Hetfeld, another Portland Pigs player, is now a successful lumber broker.

The Portland Pigs had a black pig as a mascot; her name was Gladys. Gladys was permitted out of her trailer when the team played a game at Delta Park in North Portland. Gladys would roam around the park and, instead of "rooting" for the team during the game, she would "root" in the shrubs totally oblivious to the action taking place on the field. Gladys was well traveled and even went as far as northern California to inspire the team. Unfortunately, Gladys developed a slight weight problem—a 300 lb. weight problem. Coupled with the fact that she wasn't proving to be the best mascot, poor Gladys was barbecued one summer day on a small farm near Portland. Out of respect for Gladys, quite a number of the Portland Pig rugby players were present as it was a free lunch on Gladys. Later, my son told me that he and Harvey Hetfeld just didn't have the heart to attend Gladys' barbecue. (My keen investigative intuition tells me that it had more to do with the fact that they had both had a late lunch that day.)

I recall one case where Michael Shinn sent me to find a witness in one of his civil cases. I went to a small town near Portland, checked around and found out where the witness was supposedly living. It was one of those addresses where you drive to a red barn, turn left at the cemetery, go up a hill, turn right, and take a dirt road through the woods. I drove about a mile through a thick wooded area before I came to an open spot on a hillside. I slowly drove out of the woods and approached the yard of a beautiful home. I looked up at the deck of the house and saw six ladies sunbathing in the nude. The ladies did not notice me because I was more or less between the trees. I did not know what to do. After collecting my thoughts, I decided that I would drive back into the woods and then make another approach honking my horn. However, as I was backing up, the ladies saw me, and ran into the house screaming. A lady appeared a few minutes later—*wearing clothes.* She was somewhat irritated and mumbling something about the gate not being locked. She was helpful, and told me that the witness I was looking for could be found through a police officer in a small nearby town.

I went to the police station and ran into a buzz saw disguised in a policeman's uniform. The policeman was not happy, attributing this to a lot of internal problems at the station. He was rather gruff but, under the circumstances, I did not blame him. He finally gave me the name of another person who could help me.

The third trip on this case took me to a poor rural area in the hilly country northwest of Portland. The address boasted an overgrown yard, a run-down house and one very big Rottweiler on the porch. The dog and I eyed each other for a few moments and, finally, I decided to go for the door. I have run into a lot of dogs in my travels and I like dogs. Generally, I believe that dogs sense this, but this Rottweiler was different. I got out of my car and had only walked about five feet when the big dog came running at me full steam ahead. He was snarling and barking and showing every sharp tooth in that mouth of his. I gave ground and made a mad dash back to my car. Just as I closed the door, the Rottweiler leaped on the hood and continued to "show me his smile" through the windshield. Finally, the owner of the house appeared and said he didn't think the dog would have attacked me if I had not made such a hasty retreat to the car. The dog and I eyed each other both knowing this wasn't true. In any event, I obtained the out-of-state address of the witness and my assignment was completed.

In a later conversation with Michael, he jokingly remarked about the way I had handled the assignment. In turn, I jokingly told Michael, "Look, you gave me an assignment and the first thing that happened was you sent me to a house full of mad and nude women. I just about got shot because they thought I was a Peeping Tom. Then, I had to go to a Fort Apache police station. Finally, a Rottweiler wanted to have me for lunch. Michael, if these are the kinds of cases you want me to work, I'm going to have to raise my rates to cover hazardous duty."

Michael's lightening response was: "Instead of giving you extra hazard pay, I'll give you a car phone so that you can call me for immediate assistance in tough situations—like when you saw the six nude ladies on the deck."

I worked another case for Michael involving a pickup and a logging truck. Unfortunately, the two young people in the pickup were killed. My need to obtain firsthand background information on the two youngsters killed in the accident took me to a commune where they had lived. The building that housed the commune was about five miles from the closest highway and stood by a stream in a thick stand of fir trees. It was a very dark and moonless night and quite late when I arrived. I have never been treated nicer than I was by the young people of this commune. The men wore beards and the ladies were dressed in long flowered dresses. After finishing my interviews, they offered me some health cookies and a cup of herbal tea. Because it was very late, they asked me to stay the night in one of their extra bedrooms. I declined their kind offer, after which one of them followed me out to the highway so I would not get lost in the woods. As I was driving back to Portland, I thought about what a nice group of youngsters they were, and how fortunate I was to have visited them. I learned a valuable lesson—never be judgmental of any group until you know them; you may be able to learn a great deal from one another.

I enjoyed working for Michael. Other cases I investigated for him involved sexual harassment, murder and personal injuries. Michael is an atorney who does very well working difficult cases.

WILDERNESS LIVING

Thinking of my visit to the commune reminded me of a case where I had to contact a former extra gang laborer on the railroad. This young man lived with a young woman in the wilds of northern Idaho. They lived in a rustic log cabin he had built in a remote area surrounded by pine trees near a mountain stream. They had an iron barrel made into a stove for heating and cooking.

In view of their primitive existence, I questioned the young lady about her background. She told me that she had been raised in southern California and that her father was a corporate executive. I also asked her about why she had chosen to live in the wild in this rustic manner. She told me that she really enjoyed living in the forest with her companion, her goats and the wildlife. She said it was true they did not have modern conveniences, but there were other rewards — taking a bath in the clear stream, being in their warm cabin by the fire with the wind howling outside, and the snow beautifying the landscape. She said they were removed from the hassles of freeways, crime, air pollution, bills and all the selfish and self-centered people. Obviously, this woman had led quite a different life in California. I gathered it had been quite privileged. She told me how her father had bought her mother a gift—a brand new Buick. All her mother could do was complain to her companions how disappointed she was because it wasn't a Cadillac. After all, all her friends at the club drove Cadillacs.

She told me that some of the animals that came around the cabin were friendlier than her old neighbors back in California. She felt that people were too busy to enjoy life and nature because they were working so hard to make all the money they could so, that they could make even more money.

She mentioned that there were disappointments in living in the woods. She described a recent incident where a cougar killed one of their milk goats. All in all, however, she said they really enjoyed nature and its great beauty. Their main source of entertainment in the winter months was a great collection of poems and books they kept in the cabin.

I had a nice visit with this young couple and, here again, I was lucky to be treated to a wild huckleberry jam sandwich with tea. Their food supply came from a huge garden and a general store many miles away.

Northern Idaho, where this couple had decided to live, is a beautiful place. I recall driving an attorney from Minnesota to Sandpoint to interview witnesses. The attorney said that Minnesota has a thousand beautiful lakes, but that he had never seen such beautiful, clear, blue water as in the lakes we passed. I have a color photograph that actually shows the trees and the white clouds mirrored in the water of a lake.

I recall a case involving a serious railroad crossing accident in Portland where our train struck an automobile. I checked one of the witnesses who resided about thirty miles from Portland in an A-frame house on a riverbank. He was one of six adults in a communal *family*. He was also an eyewitness for the bell and whistle. When I interviewed him he told me he could see the train approaching the crossing when it was about 200 yards from the point of impact. Now, in a crossing accident it is imperative to check the crossing area prior to proceeding with the investigation. I had been to the crossing and the view showed the train could only be seen for about 100 yards from where this gentleman was standing. Rather than try to verbally convince him of the correct distance, I suggested if he had the time to drive to the scene with me, we could measure the distance and insert it in his statement. He agreed to do so even though he was going to miss out on the family dinner.

He measured the distance at the crossing and was satisfied he could see the train for the first time when it was about ninety yards away. Before driving the thirty miles back to his house, I told him I was not permitted to pay him for his time. However, in light of the fact he missed his evening dinner, I told him I could take him to a restaurant in Portland so he would not miss out on dinner. He refused to go to a restaurant and instead suggested we go to McDonald's. I thought my expense account was going to get off pretty cheap, but I was wrong. At McDonald's he ordered six hamburgers, six milkshakes, six French fries and six apples pies. He explained that his *family* had undoubtedly missed him at dinner and that it was only fair that they be included. What could I say? The deed was done. When we arrived back at the house he told me to wait in the car. They had caught a big salmon the week before and were still "working on it." He wanted me to take a piece of the salmon home with me. When I was in the house earlier that day I didn't see a refrigerator. Imagine my relief when, with a dejected look, he came back out and said, "Damn them. They ate the whole thing." He also told me that they were already enjoying the food we had brought to them as a "bonus." As it turned out, we didn't use him at trial. It was probably a good thing because he probably would have wanted to bring the entire family to trial and lunch at McDonald's.

I had an appointment with another group of flower children on a death case in Southern Oregon. I arrived early for my appointment and, after knocking on the door, I was told their Bible study meeting was just about over and I was welcome to join them. I joined the group; however, I was somewhat dismayed to find that they were all smoking pot. Pot or no pot, I must say they certainly could quote scripture.

I worked a case in Washington where two flower children, a boy and girl, were hitchhiking. Both had golden locks down to the back of their necks. A man, the only occupant in the car, stopped and picked them up thinking they were both girls. Unfortunately, the man had something else on his mind and when he realized that one of the hitchhikers was a boy, he stopped at a hamburger joint and gave the boy some money to go buy hamburgers. While the boy was buying the food, the man drove off with the girl and raped her. Fortunately, he was caught and sentenced.

One day an attorney called and said he had a dram shop case for me to investigate. Apparently, a cocktail waitress on her night off, went into the lounge where she worked. In the early morning hours, and after considerable drinking, she was driving along and went off the street striking the rear of a parked police car with two Beaverton policemen inside. The impact was severe and the two officers were taken to the hospital for whiplash treatment. The waitress did not have any insurance. In view of the fact that this woman was very intoxicated at the time of the accident, it was alleged the owner of the lounge, Mike Kosmos, had served her too much liquor.

My investigation discovered that the lady had left Mike's lounge around 11:30 P.M. and did not appear to be intoxicated. The accident occurred at 1:00 A.M. at a location approximately two miles from the lounge. Further investigation revealed that she left the lounge and went to a parking lot where she and another male customer from the lounge consumed a full bottle of whiskey while in the car. The attorney representing the police officers dropped the case once the facts of my investigation were revealed.

The owner of the lounge called and wanted to speak with me. He was extremely grateful about the case's outcome. What had made the case more difficult was that the man involved in the drinking in the parking lot was married and no one wanted to divulge his involvement in the case. In any event, Mike was grateful and we became good friends. His lounge included a stage where he had country music on weekends. He saw to it that everyone in the neighborhood enjoyed themselves—even to the extent of dancing polkas with some of the elderly women who came in without partners. Mike wanted everyone to have a good time, but ran a tight ship. Mike's place was the watering hole for many attorneys. He loved animals and it was a well-known fact that a lot of people left their stray animals at the lounge. It was not unusual to see Mike at Safeway loading up his van with cat and dog food to feed the strays left on his doorstep.

On one occasion I delivered some apples to Mike for his racehorses. I arrived as he was making their dinner—a blend of rolled oats, carrots, apples and molasses. That concoction smelled so good that it would not have been too difficult to swap lunches with the horses. These were very content horses, not necessarily great racers, but very content.

"The Green Meadows" was the meeting place for many of the notables of Washington County—county officials, law enforcement personnel, lawyers and judges. One judge told me that Mike operated a clean place and didn't have trouble at his lounge. Consequently, after bar meetings some of the attorneys and judges would gather at the Green Meadows for a beer or two. Mike, a former policeman, was also quite unique in that he was more interested in his customer's welfare than most businessmen. He closed on Sundays and Mondays so his employees could be with their families on Sundays and have two days off in a row. Unfortunately, the Green Meadows was torn down and another business is in its place.

RICHARD AUSTRIA

The Austria case was one of the largest single personal injury cases I ever investigated. John and Pearl Austria came to this country in 1972 from the Philippines where they graduated from a university in Manila. One child, Noel, had already been born. Within a month of arriving here, John put his accounting degree to good use and hired out as an accountant for an insurance company. Later, Pearl went to work for the Owens Corning Company in the quality control department. They worked hard and were able to purchase a nice home in the Gresham area. Two children followed Noel—Theresa and Richard. John and Pearl appreciated being in America to raise and educate their children. Life for them was good.

Then tragedy struck when Richard was seriously injured while playing high school football. This episode brought back memories of my mother. She told me when I was a small boy after someone killed my dog that everyone, no matter how rich, how educated, or how handsome or beautiful would have a taste of good life and at times there would be bad times—that this was a part of life.

At the time of Richard's accident, Noel and Theresa were both enrolled in universities. Richard was a junior at Gresham High School in 1985; all three were excellent students. Richard had expressed a desire to be a surgeon. Fate, however, did not see it that way. He had all the qualifications for success—he was an exceptional student, president of the junior class and admired and respected by his peers.

During my investigation I spoke to many of Richard's classmates. One of them told me she had a friend in Richard; that she had a rough life and some of the students would avoid her because she lived on the wrong side of the tracks. Richard was not like the other students. He always had a smile for her and stopped and talked with her, making her feel much better. He was always assisting others.

His teachers told me they were gearing up his class schedules with subjects that would help him in his medical studies later.

Richard played basketball and in his freshman year he approached his parents and asked them if he could play football. His father and mother took into consideration that Richard was of slight build and only weighed about 140 lbs. They suggested that Richard not play because of his size. In his sophomore year Richard again asked permission to play football and again they denied his request. In his junior year Richard tried another approach. He pointed out to his parents that he was a good student, president of his class, that he was the first one up every Sunday morning to get everybody up for church, and that he never caused any problems. He continued by saying that if they loved him, they would permit him to play football. The weight problem must have been in the minds of the jury at the time of trial; however, when the above information was brought out it appeared it was something they could understand.

Richard went on to play football in his junior year. This was in September of 1985. He was sixteen and playing on the second team as a linebacker where the coach had placed him because of his quickness and intelligence. During one practice in September the coach announced that he was concluding practice when a 210 lb., hard-running and speedy fullback made a request for one last special play before practice ended. He wanted to run another play with the ball on the two-yard line. He said he wanted to go over the top—over the other players and over the goal line. The coach consented to his request. Richard and the fullback collided in mid-air after which the fullback failed to cross the goal line. A few minutes later the coach singled out Richard to the other players and told them that if he continued to play with the same determination he had just shown on that play, he would be starting with the varsity.

Richard was dazed by the collision but was able to walk off the field seemingly having suffered no ill effects. Approximately two weeks later, he experienced severe headaches. On October 1, 1985, Richard collapsed during football practice. A CT scan showed that he had a subdural hematoma. Dr. Lawrence Frank, an excellent surgeon, operated but, as the result of his injuries, Richard suffered a catastrophic brain injury that also resulted in severe physical impairment. Strenuous physical and speech therapy followed and Richard continues to receive these treatments to this day—fifteen years later. He has treatments three times a week; Richard's father drives him about 100 miles on each trip.

John and Pearl have patiently devoted their lives to the care of Richard. One would not be wrong in saying the accident had a terrible impact on Richard, John and Pearl. During the day a nurse's aide assists Pearl in Richard's care.

The investigation of Richard's case commenced with the coaches and any possibility their negligence contributed to this accident. My investigation revealed their coaching expertise in no way contributed to the accident. Other aspects of the case were investigated with negative results. I recall a meeting with Jim and Mark in which we discussed the possibility that the equipment was in some way defective. I picked up all of the football equipment Richard was wearing at the time of the accident.

After examining the equipment, particularly the helmet, Jim and Mark suspected there was a weakness on one side of the helmet. This turned out to be the main issue at the three-week trial. Jim and Mark did a masterful job in serving numerous subpoenas on the company that manufactured the helmet. It was revealed that they had problems in testing this particular size helmet and that the entire forehead region of the helmet was deficient. Unfortunately, Richard just happened to be struck on the left front area of his helmet. One of the big questions was whether the helmet's front sizer (foam rubber piece) found in the area where the fullback's knee had impacted was adequate and met existing safety standards. Evidence was introduced as to how Richard was struck, and what a football helmet is supposed to do to reduce the impact of a collision. The injury to Richard's head was precisely the kind of injury that a helmet is designed to prevent.

This issue was bitterly fought over at the time of trial. It was revealed many tests had been conducted on this helmet because there was a question as to its safety. In checking further, we found four death cases involving this particular helmet. No previous lawsuits had been filed in these deaths, however, because the time for filing suit had expired.

Mark Bocci and Jim Pippin tried the case on behalf of the Austria family and the helmet manufacturer hired three attorneys, one from Seattle and two from back east. The Eastern lawyers had fine law school backgrounds along with very good reputations for trying cases. As the trial progressed it was amazing to see half of the courtroom filed with insurance managers, lawyers and legal secretaries—all working for the defense. I was the only one in the seating area on our side. The jury got to look upon a David and Goliath picture for the entire two-week trial.

During the trial it was my responsibility to have the witnesses available when it came time for them to testify and be on hand to support the attorneys in any way I could. I was also to be with Richard's parents during the trial to answer their questions and ensure that their behavior was proper. The latter was totally unnecessary because they conducted themselves perfectly.

After a verdict in the case was brought in, the defense alleged Pearl and a member of the jury had had some type of contact. This turned out to be entirely false and I pointed out that I was very observant of their exceptional good conduct during the trial in an affidavit. To illustrate this we never rode in the same elevator with anyone on the jury. If we spotted the jury seated at a table when we entered a restaurant, we would immediately walk out of that restaurant and go to another, as we did not want any eye contact whatsoever with them.

Mark Bocci and Jim Pippin are two very compassionate attorneys. When the jury was out in the Austria case we went to dinner and discussed the case and the possible outcome. This type of get-together gives the attorneys time to think what they should or should not have done during the trial. A great deal of Monday morning quarterbacking goes on. These two attorneys put up over $300,000 to try the case. Mark and Sheri Bocci sold their home in order to raise sufficient funds to pursue this case. How many professional people put up this kind of money with the possibility of losing it, notwithstanding the enormous amount of time that was spent in handling the case? A case of this kind is an immense emotional and financial investment. During our conversation at dinner Mark said, "You know, Lou, if the jury brings in a verdict against Richard we will be set back big time, but we will eventually be back, and life will go on for all of us." Jim and he then stated that the only problem was who was going to take care of Richard, and the concern about the tremendous future medical expenses and intensive care he must have if a jury does not bring in a verdict for him. It was very humbling to listen to these two powerful litigators who had spent vast amounts of their own money and worked so hard with such passion, express even more concern about who was going to take care of Richard than anything else.

Fortunately, the jury came back and returned a verdict for $11.3 million dollars. Two years later the verdict was affirmed by an appellate court and paid in full, plus interest. Some people have said the verdict was excessive. However, this can best be answered by Richard's mother, Pearl, and his father who stated on a number of occasions that they would gladly give all the judgment money back and all of their own money to have Richard the way he was before the injury. The defective helmet certainly changed the entire course of all of their lives. Fate deals a bad hand at times, and instead of Richard possibly being a skilled surgeon and helping others, he must have constant care. I hope medical science will someday be able to bring him back at least partially recovered.

To this day, Jim, Mark and I are very concerned about Richard's problems. We were deeply touched when his father recently told us that they did not consider us friends— that they considered us family.

On our last visit the nurse told me Richard had made a surprising statement to her that morning just out of the clear blue. He said, "Today is going to be a great day for me." She asked him why he felt that way and he answered that friends were coming to see him. You can't put a dollar value on things like that.

There is no question that money is an issue, but it also reflects on the question, "Would you give up your eyesight for all the jewels in the world?" The answer, of course, is obvious. We have been working on John and Pearl to spend more time by themselves and, even though they tell us they will, they never do. They are no longer employed outside the home—they give their everything to Richard and we have a tremendous amount of admiration for them.

Regardless of Richard's twelve years of progress, John and Pearl cannot forget how Richard was before the accident. He used to come home from school, take a nap until about four o'clock in the afternoon and then study until midnight. "Richard would check all the windows and doors to make sure all was safe. He would then look into my bedroom to see if I was all right. I miss that. We still have our hopes. We want him back," John says. Richard continues to improve through great effort. At first, he was only able to write the first four letters of his name and he has now mastered writing his complete name. John and Pearl recognize that Richard may need twenty-four-hour care for the rest of his life, but they are still hoping for a miraculous recovery. "You know how parents are—they never give up, and we want him back," says John.

There's an unbelievable amount of money in professional sports. I would like to see some of that money channeled to establish a fund to assist seriously injured high school athletes. High schools are the training grounds of professional athletes and those athletes should be protected too. I understand that high school insurance for athletes at times is not sufficient for injuries of a very serious nature.

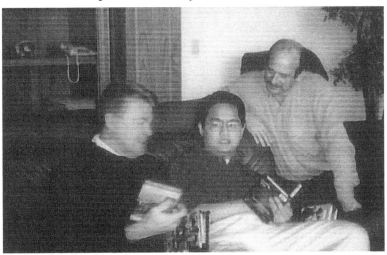

Taken during the Christmas holidays in 1999, this picture show Jim Pippin, Richard Austria, and Mark Bocci (left to right). Jim and Mark are presenting gifts to Richard. Even though Richard's trial has been over for 10 years, these attorneys are very much concerned about Richard's health and welfare. The visits have continued throughout the years and they have been enjoyed by all. Jim and Mark had no knowledge that this photograph would be publicized.

Frank Lude, a former U.S. Marshall, and me.
Frank told me that Mrs. Nixon was a wonderful person and
that she would take the marshals' wives and their children to
breakfast when they were out of town with the President. (1998)

ATTORNEYS

I understand there are a million attorneys in our country and about 13,000 of them are in the State of Oregon. Throughout my fifty-year career of conducting investigations and settling cases, I have worked with attorneys in Seattle, Omaha, Spokane, Kansas City, Portland and other cities. The majority of them are skillful, honest, knowledgeable and, most certainly, hard working. I am not painting all attorneys with the same brush. They fall in the same category as in any other occupations. There is a very high percentage of good ones and a very small percentage of bad ones. Of course, you hear more about the bad ones and very little, if anything, about the good ones.

I rarely ran into an attorney that I did not like. However, I recall one case where an attorney (more or less a previous co-worker) had a case involving a member of his family. I worked the investigation of the case that involved driving fifty miles on weekends late at night to contact midnight employee witnesses at a hospital. At first, because of our slight relationship, I was not going to charge him for the investigation, but then I decided I would charge him half my normal fee. The case was settled quite some time afterwards for a six-figure amount. I certainly did not expect any additional money, but I was disappointed that the attorney did not thank me for the work I had done.

There was another attorney I worked for who sued an elderly couple I believed was in no way responsible for an accident. After the attorney filed the suit, I questioned him as to why he had sued them in view of the fact he had agreed with me beforehand that there was no liability on the elderly couple's part. His answer was that the defendant would settle the case on a nuisance basis. After this one case, I refused to work for this attorney. The elderly couple was very nice and scared to death they would be sued.

Cases like that are quite rare and, as I have stated, the vast majority of the 200 attorneys I worked for were just great. They have worked long and hard to gain the skills and knowledge necessary to provide the quality representation their clients deserve.

I really don't believe the layperson understands the amount of work an attorney performs to handle a trial from the beginning to the end. It is simply immense. A great number of trials commence on a Monday morning and this timing robs the attorney of time for himself or with his family on weekends. Long hours are spent preparing opening and closing arguments, talking to witnesses, studying the law, making motions that become involved in the case, filing briefs, etc. etc. During many trials I stayed with attorneys until late at night in hotel rooms discussing the case with witnesses, talking to and locating new witnesses to confront evidence given during the trial. The attorneys spend hours and hours after each day of the trial preparing for facts and points that have come up or may come up unexpectedly during the trial. Whether on offense or defense, a truly good trial lawyer has to be a jack-of-all-trades and must match his intelligence with all types of expert witnesses, judges and his opponent. These witnesses have electrical engineering, mechanical engineering, psychiatry and medical degrees. He must have a thorough knowledge of the medical profession because in most personal injury cases there is always considerable disputed testimony about the medical aspect of the case. An attorney has to have at least equal knowledge of a subject as an expert to bring out the facts for the benefit of his client.

Both attorneys walk a tightrope during a trial. If one slips, the other is certain to grab the opportunity. It's just those kinds of slips that can have great significance on the outcome of any trial. There's always a question of whether to present a witness in a case. Consideration must be given beforehand whether the witness will make a good witness or a bad one. They also must decide whether a witness should be brought back on rebuttal or be released.

It is always a question mark how a particular witness will perform on the stand in front of a jury. I recall a witness testifying in a trial concerning the speed of a car prior to a collision with a train at a railroad crossing. The plaintiff's attorney talked to the witness prior to the trial and the latter told him that he would estimate the speed of the car to be about 40 mph. The attorney then brought out the fact that this was within the speed limit. At the trial, the plaintiff's attorney questioned the witness as to the speed of the car. Instead of answering the questions as he had previously, 40 mph, the witness testified, "That car was coming down the hill like a hummingbird through a tulip patch." The attorney then attempted to repair the damage and, although the witness pointed out he had previously said 40 mph, this was too fast when approaching a railroad crossing. Perhaps the answer could have been avoided by asking the witness the rate of speed in the area and dropping the matter.

As to expert witnesses, attorney Mark Bocci had a case involving a serious personal injury that occurred in a motorcycle accident. The defense's expert witness was a college professor with a degree in mechanical engineering; he was an expert on motorcycles. The engineer was considered one of the best and was brought out from the East Coast for the trial. After the engineer's testimony on the stand, Mark said it would be necessary for us to find a witness who would have a different version about how the mechanical part would operate. My problem was where to find one when one of the best in the country had already testified for the defense. Mark suggested an expert motorcycle mechanic might fit the bill, and we finally found one in Eastern Oregon. The man had about twenty-five years of experience repairing motorcycles. Boy, what a witness he made. He was a good-looking biker and gave the impression that he could make a Harley talk. We knew we had a good one when the defense attorney questioned him about his opinion on how a certain part of a motorcycle operated. His answer was, "I don't have opinions—I know what I am talking about." Many members of the jury smiled and it was obvious the witness rang a bell.

I recall another excellent witness who could barely speak English. An attorney asked him what he had seen and heard at the time of the accident. The manner in which the witness answered the question was not to the attorney's liking. He asked the witness if he recalled their conversation a week before when he stated this and that. The witness answered him with, "I no saya that. You want me to saya that, but I no saya that." A college professor could not have been a better witness.

It bothers me when I hear people say they don't understand how attorneys can act like real enemies when they are in the courtroom, and then turn right around and go out for lunch together and be buddy-buddy. What's wrong with that if they give it their best shot in the courtroom? I see no difference between that and two boxers trying to knock the stuffing out of each other, and when the fight is over, they hug in the middle of the ring.

Burl Green, a legendary attorney in his time, tangled on many occasions with Walter Cosgrave, another legend in the Portland area. When these two attorneys faced each other in the courtroom the fur would really fly. Yet, these two men regularly played golf together. Their battles in the courtroom were so intense that usually both were so angry they would not play golf with each other for a month or two. Then, calm would return, they would make up and resume playing golf together until the next trial. It was more or less a standing joke in the legal community whether sufficient time had passed for the two of them to make up and play golf. There is no way this was an act. These men were very highly respected for their integrity.

In another case two attorneys got into a heated argument during a trial. After the trial our attorney was still so angry that he asked if he could ride back with me instead of with the other attorney. It simply isn't true that all attorneys act the big fight. For the most part, the feelings displayed in the courtroom are real and sincere. The average layperson just isn't aware of the attorneys' feelings after he/she has spent a day in court, and had been up half the night working on a case. Attorneys also try not to lose their temper in court because they know it may cost points with the jury.

There is also a misconception that attorneys charge too much and they all make obscene amounts of money on their cases. Not true. The attorney may spend considerable time and money on a case and then lose it all when a jury comes in with a "goose egg" verdict, or worse yet, on appeal. The average small-town attorney usually charges $150 per hour when consulted. He has to pay federal and state income taxes, office help, office rent, use of an automobile, insurance and many other expenses such as utilities, office machinery, licenses, legal publications and continuing legal education. Not much of that $150 is left.

I have a friend in Denver who has an income of $18,000 a month from one of his many rental buildings who complains that attorneys are robbers and is pretty vocal about it. There are attorneys, a very small percentage, who make millions of dollars, but you do not hear about the ones who just make a decent living. I would think if people want to complain about someone making millions of dollars they wouldn't have to look any farther than the athletes who get paid for hitting a ball with a stick or bouncing a ball on a court. Being paid $130,000 to play in one basketball game is a lot of money.

I have friends who complain about the big fees attorneys receive at the cigarette trials, but these same people have no problem paying $200 for tickets, $10 for parking, $25 for refreshments, etc. when they take their family to a sporting event.

When I hear about people complaining about the high charges of an attorney, I think of the company that sent over a man to fix my plugged sink. He charged me $110 for about ten minutes of work. Compare the education requirements between the two professions.

Only the big-dollar verdicts are published in the papers because it makes news but, unfortunately, it gives the public the impression that all attorneys are in this classification. Even these attorneys do not have the money in hand, since almost all these big awards are appealed. Appeals require even more work and there is always the possibility of the verdict being overturned.

I like to think that attorneys are providing a service, like scientists, doctors, educators and others. Where would we be if we didn't have attorneys and judges to interpret the laws of the land?

As I mentioned earlier, the good work of attorneys is usually not publicized. For example, I investigated a case for Jim Pippin. My investigation revealed an elderly man involved in an alleged fraudulent case. Although cleared of criminal charges, he left himself wide open for a civil case. The facts revealed that he needed money for a cancer problem. His wife had left him, he had been fired after working at one firm for a number of years, and had lost his pension. After discussing this information with Jim he said although there was some money in the case, the man had suffered enough, and he picked up my investigation file and dropped it into a wastepaper basket. This is something you don't read in the newspaper about attorneys. What you read in the newspaper is the case in Washington where a man drinking at a bar went downstairs to the restroom, fell and injured his back. The papers publicized in headlines that the man received a verdict of $100,000 from a jury when the plaintiff was drinking at a bar. They publicized it as one of the biggest verdicts in the history of that county. What they didn't print was that a year later the case was reversed by an Appellate Court and the plaintiff received nothing. People have a tendency to use this information to reinforce their belief that their own personal case is worth more because they have a more serious injury and they were not drinking when they were injured. Attorneys are blamed for excessive verdicts; however, if the case is ultimately appraised incorrectly the responsibility should fall on the jury—not the attorney. It is up to the attorney to do the best job possible for his client and then it is left to the jury to make any final decision.

Attorneys are also blamed when a felon is successfully defended and is set free. It is important to remember that, just as in a civil matter, it is up to the defense attorney to do the best possible job for his client, but the jury has the final say. If a wrong verdict was rendered in the O.J. Simpson trial, it was not the fault of his attorney, Johnny Cochran, but the fault of the jury who delivered the verdict.

It is said that an attorney will take any type of a case. Most of the time it is not the attorney who wants to take on a case, but the client who insists that he do so. It's kind of like the contractor who needs work and is approached by someone to build a house with an odd looking roof. The contractor can advise him that this is certainly not practical, but if the client insists should he turn it down? The client has the ultimate control to hire and fire his attorney.

Settlement of cases just prior to or at the time of trial presents attorneys with a big problem. It's not knowing whether a jury is going to return a "goose egg" verdict, or render a large verdict that's so difficult to deal with. When relaying an offer that is rejected, many attorneys require their client to sign papers stating that they rejected the offer. This can come into play if the jury brings in an amount much more than the original offer. I recall one case where the defendant's attorney would not accept a settlement offer of $1 million and the jury awarded $8 million.

Actually, settlement discussions are like a poker game with the same result—someone loses and someone wins. Let's say a jury awards $100,000 in punitive damages and $25,000 in special damages. Out of the $100,000 punitive damages the State of Oregon receives sixty percent and the plaintiff and attorney split the remaining forty percent and each receive $20,000. The Internal Revenue Service then takes its cut out of the amounts awarded to the plaintiff and the attorney. What other profession or business is required to pay sixty percent of their profit to the State?

Although not every case involves punitive damages, they can serve a purpose in creating safety measures for the general population. A manufacturer of children's clothing used 100% cotton that was not flame-retardant. The company stopped making garments in 1980 when a jury ordered it to pay punitive damages to a four-year old girl who was very badly burned when her blouse caught fire. It is interesting to note that, according to a 1990 study, punitive damages are only awarded in less than five percent of jury verdicts.

I have worked for many good and honorable insurance companies. However, some are the first to complain about the numerous lawsuits costing the policyholder more money. This may be true, but in some ways they have brought this on themselves. When working in Spokane an insurance company ran an ad showing a non-invitee (door-to-door salesman) slipping on a homeowner's icy porch. The ad went on to tell how you can be sued big time for this sort of thing and to buy their insurance for protection. Doesn't this sort of promotion give certain people the idea that they can sue for something like this?

When I first started in the business years ago, I disliked lawsuits so much that I became pretty vocal about it. This went on until one day my supervisor asked me where I thought I would be working if lawsuits were prohibited. For the first time I was aware that this is all a part of our system. Where would defense attorneys be working if plaintiffs did not file lawsuits?

There are quite a number of people who are very critical of our justice system and of our attorneys. If they would stop and think, they would recognize the fine quality of justice that comes out of our system. Not every case is perfect, and some will argue it is not the best, but in reality it is the best we have until something better comes along. Most of the public is not aware that out of the total number of lawsuits filed in our state courts, only about five percent are personal injury lawsuits. Out of that five percent, only a small fraction can be called frivolous. Most of the court suits involve divorces, bankruptcies, business problems, criminal and other types of lawsuits. Why do the personal injury cases get more attention? The answer is that the news media know it is far more interesting to read about a dog biting a man in the buttocks or a golf ball hitting a tree, bouncing off onto someone's head. These are actual cases and are far more entertaining than following cases involving infringements of rights, products liability or other business disputes.

Lawsuits are actually important in our life, and settle many issues peacefully. Without lawsuits some cases could be disastrous if handled in another manner—think of people and shotguns. I worked a case in Eastern Oregon where two neighbors got to a point where they were shooting at each other's barn with rifles over water rights. Finally, I arranged for an impartial judge and they reluctantly agreed to accept his decision. This ended the dispute.

Perhaps if the Hatfields and McCoys had ironed out their original problem in court, the long-lasting feud between the families and thirty-eight deaths could have been avoided.

I have heard individuals say on many occasions that they do not like attorneys defending criminals when there is strong evidence that the individual is guilty. At one time I felt the same way, but we have to recognize that there have been defendants found guilty and sentenced to death where DNA tests now reveal they were innocent. As much as I loathe someone murdering another human being, it also affects me the same way when a defendant is wrongly convicted and sentenced to death for a crime he or she did not commit. What is hardly ever mentioned or revealed is how many lives have been saved and how many prison terms have been eliminated by attorneys who successfully defend a person charged with a crime he or she didn't commit. There are probably cases where a guilty person was found innocent, but we can't have it both ways.

If those who complain about attorneys find a better way of adjudicating the law and preserving our freedom, let them come forth. Attorneys Thomas Jefferson and Abraham Lincoln were extremely diligent in preserving our freedom. Some of my friends criticize attorneys for defending criminals or people accused of committing crimes. Numerous people criticize an attorney for advertising on television and radio. Why shouldn't they? They have the same right as anyone else to advertise their services.

People often ask me if I prefer to work for plaintiff or defense attorneys. I would have to say that I make no distinction. I have enjoyed working with both and only require that the attorneys I work for be honest and conscientious.

FINAL RETIREMENT

I'm eighty years old at this writing and it has been an interesting exercise to look back and document my life, its accomplishments and its setbacks.

I recall the schoolteacher who long ago told me that we are here for such a short time that our lives would be wasted if we didn't work at a job we enjoy. Well, I was fortunate and found working as an investigator for fifty years to be personally and professionally rewarding. I considered each case a puzzle to be solved, and I was always focused on finding the answer to the puzzle.

It's tragic that we are only on this sweet earth for such a short time. When it's time for me to travel "upstairs" to meet my blessed maker, I hope someone greets me at the gate and hands me a typewriter and some cases to investigate.

Personal Acknowledgments

I would like to acknowledge the following individuals for the important part each has played in my life:

Monte Bricker
A real vigorous take-charge lawyer and an admirable negotiating adversary. We had many heated arguments over the years, but I will never forget his thoughtfulness in taking time off from his busy schedule to visit me at the hospital when I had a serious heart problem. It was back to business as usual when I was released from the hospital.

Austin W. Crowe, Jr.
I assisted Austin when he won the first railroad case he ever tried. I was asked about his performance afterwards and I answered, "There is no question he is going to be a very good one." I was certainly proven right over the years.

Carol Foley
A peach of a lady. She is not only my insurance counselor, but is a very good friend as well. Her answers to technical insurance questions have always been right on. She also has more common sense than many people I know.

Anthony Furniss
I investigated a number of cases for Anthony, including an alleged murder case. He is a skilled attorney and is very conscientious. He worries that he isn't doing enough for his clients. Anthony suggested I write a book based on the statements I took for him.

Richard Gemson
A Seattle attorney who was the Rock of Gibraltar as a defense attorney for the railroad. He once sent me to the county jail to interview a witness after which he called to ask if I had any trouble getting out of jail. He has a good sense of humor, but is very serious when it comes to practicing law.

Fred Gilbert
A partner in a large law firm in Spokane. Excellent trial lawyer, now retired. He tried many cases for the railroad in the Yakima and Walla Walla areas.

Roland Haacke
Now a retired Union Pacific employee. A real cultured gentleman. Graduated from Princeton in engineering. He provided valuable advice when I had engineering problems in cases and became a valued friend.

Terry Hall
A capable well-rounded attorney in Hillsboro. He did an excellent job when he represented a family whose four-year-old was severely burned in a gasoline explosion in the laundry room of an apartment complex. He has a good sense of humor and I enjoyed working for him.

Herb Hamlen, deceased
An Abe Lincoln type of lawyer from Spokane. The first attorney I worked for over forty years ago. He was sharp in his arguments and very appealing to a jury. An honorable civic-minded gentleman. I was fortunate to gain experience from his knowledge of conducting investigations and this later assisted me in being promoted to Kansas City. He won ten cases in a row during the five years I was in Spokane.

Carl and Linda Hawker

I have known Carl and Linda (Lin) for many years and consider myself fortunate to call them friends. Carl is a top-notch investigator who I first met when we worked together at the railroad. Lin has consistently encouraged me to complete this project and participated in its production.

Randall B. Kester

A very knowledgeable and solid lawyer and a former Oregon Supreme Court Justice. He was a Union Pacific Railroad general solicitor for many years. Now retired, he is back to being a partner in a Portland law firm. Randall is a real jewel and a gentleman. He always had time no matter how busy he was to advise me on legal issues. His door was always open to me and I owe him a great deal.

Rudy Lachenmeier

A thoughtful lawyer who I never had the pleasure to meet. He was one of four defense attorneys I worked for on a joint case. I want to thank him for a nice letter he wrote about my investigation of a delicate case involving minors who made an X-rated movie. After the case was completed, one of the attorneys asked me if I knew why I was chosen to investigate the case for them. I innocently said I did not know but deep down, I thought to myself they must have hired me because they felt I was a pretty good investigator. He then deflated my balloon by saying, with a grin, the reason I was selected was because I had that "fatherly" look.

James Logan

An astute and well informed lawyer in Kansas City. He authored articles for various law magazines. He was a judge and then returned to private practice. I worked with him for five years and really enjoyed working with him and visiting his home on the lake on many occasions. He is a very thorough lawyer.

Wm. Freming Nielsen
With Federal Judge Nielsen on the bench—justice is in wonderful hands.

Beth Perkins/Peggy Ross
Two jewels in a crown. Employed by Pippin & Bocci. Very pleasurable to work with and extremely helpful. Peggy even rototilled a garden area for my sister. The amazing thing about her rototiller was when her husband, Robert or I would put our hands on the handles it would stop. When Peggy placed her hands on the handles it would start again. Obviously, the rototiller had been programmed to perform for only Peggy.

Robert Perkins
A young attorney who employed me to investigate a number of cases. He is well versed in the law and a treat to work for.

Hollie Pihl
I have known Circuit Court Judge Hollie Pihl for many years. He has provided invaluable advice on outside legal matters. When he is not in the courtroom rendering good justice, he is out using a chainsaw on his timber ranch.

Pippin & Bocci
What else can I say other than, "I love 'em. I love 'em."

Douglas Spencer
I worked with Douglas Spencer, a Hillsboro attorney. I sent him a case where a small attractive waitress was accused of assaulting her big boyfriend by beating him up. She was very pleased with Doug's handling of her case and gave Doug and me dinner certificates. I told Doug that it was a good thing he won her case or both of us would have had to go into a Bruce Lee stance with her.

William Walsh, deceased
A senior partner in a giant law firm in Seattle and a darn good trial lawyer. Will always remember the excellent lunches Mrs. Walsh prepared for us to eat at an outdoor park in Tacoma. To get away from the trial at the courthouse during the lunch hour we went to the park where we were not disturbed. During the trial Mr. Walsh accused me of being more concerned about what Mrs. Walsh had prepared for our lunches than what was going on at the trial.

Jack Wright
Thanks for being my friend for sixty years.

Co-workers
I am filled with gratitude when I think of the countless individuals and fellow employees I have come to know throughout my investigative career. I have been rewarded with their friendship. There are too many to mention, but they know who they are.